relaxed
COASTAL
STYLE

relaxed
COASTAL
STYLE

SALLY DENNING

photography BENJAMIN EDWARDS

RYLAND PETERS & SMALL
LONDON • NEW YORK

Senior designer Megan Smith
Senior commissioning editor Annabel Morgan
Location research Jess Walton
Production manager Gordana Simakovic
Art director Leslie Harrington
Editorial director Julia Charles
Publisher Cindy Richards

First published in 2018 by
Ryland Peters & Small
20–21 Jockey's Fields
London WC1R 4BW
and
341 E 116th Street
New York, NY 10029
www.rylandpeters.com

10 9 8 7 6 5 4 3 2 1

ISBN 978-1-84975-962-5

A CIP record for this book is available
from the British Library.

Library of Congress CIP data has been
applied for.

Printed and bound in China

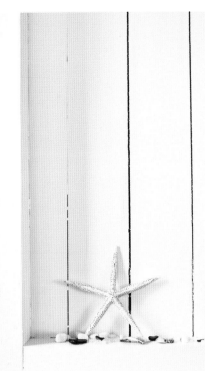
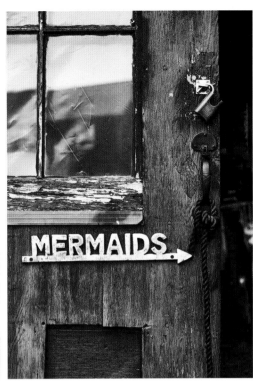

CONTENTS

INTRODUCTION

I love the sea. I love being by it, swimming in it and the way it makes me feel.
It recharges my batteries and rejuvenates me every time I visit. As a child, I was
lucky enough to spend lots of time near the coast and my father loved sailing,
so I spent a lot of time on boats. I guess you could say it's in my blood.

But I'm not unusual: the sea seems to hold an appeal for everyone, whether
it's due to the water, the clarity of the light, the scent of ozone, the sea air or the
sound of the waves crashing on the shore. Whatever its attraction, the ocean is
synonymous with restoration and revitalization.

Many of us dream of living by the sea, but *Relaxed Coastal Style* isn't intended
solely for those who are fortunate enough to have a seaside home – it shows how
to take inspiration from the beauty of the coast and bring those ideas inside

wherever and however you live. In the first part of the book, 'Coastal Elements', I look at colour palettes and textures, drawing inspiration from the natural colours of the ocean as well as the textures of weathered wood, bare floorboards, sun-bleached fabrics and robust linens. I also look at dressing windows and choosing lighting and furniture, as well as how to curate and display decorative accents such as navigation charts, maps and other nauticalia alongside shells, driftwood and beachcombing finds. The second part, 'Coastal Hideaways' explores 13 varied coastal houses around the world, all guaranteed to inspire and enchant with ideas that are transferable to any interior, whatever its location.

I hope that *Relaxed Coastal Style* will encourage you to capture the carefree, relaxed and practical spirit of the coastal home.

coastal
ELEMENTS

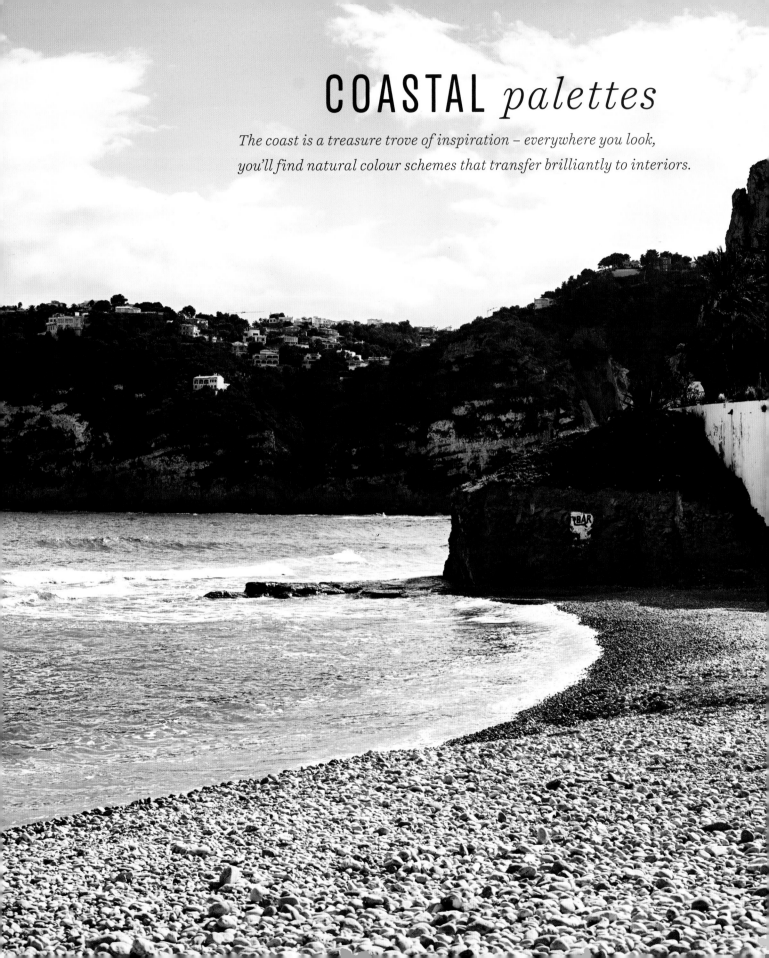

COASTAL *palettes*

The coast is a treasure trove of inspiration – everywhere you look,
you'll find natural colour schemes that transfer brilliantly to interiors.

COOL & CALMING

ALL IS SERENE.
For a peaceful feel, combine plain linens and woven furniture in light tones that have an affinity with one another, then add wooden pieces with natural or weathered finishes (opposite). Most sofa manufacturers offer a selection of linen-upholstered sofas. Loose covers/slipcovers are practical, as they can be removed and washed in the machine. Add patterned fabrics in pale colours – Jane Churchill is a great place for these. Ceramics with a handmade feel will ensure the look doesn't become too polished (above). Try local galleries for unique ceramics, but you can pick up affordable finds at stores like John Lewis, Pottery Barn or Target.

Possibly the most obvious colour palette when it comes to coastal interiors is one that's calming – the sea is synonymous with relaxation and tranquillity, after all. But it can be hard to pull off. A palette combining off-whites or pale neutrals is a good place to start. This room (opposite) shows that adding neutral upholstery, loose woven throws and cushions in two different patterns – a soft aqua ditsy print and a larger, light rust design – makes for a room that's restful yet still interesting and inviting. If possible, open up walls or ceilings and make the most of any beams or other architectural features. Or try fitting tongue-and-groove panelling to the walls to add visual interest. Finish off with pale-coloured rugs with a textured weave or subtle pattern, so that nothing becomes too overpowering.

COASTAL BRIGHTS

If you're a lover of strong colour and want to explore the bolder end of the spectrum, a coastal house can be the perfect place to do it. If you don't have a home by the sea, you can still use bright colours – it's just a case of getting the balance right so that the palette fits with your surroundings. In this Spanish beach house (above left), the vivid turquoise of the window frame works brilliantly because it coordinates with the sea beyond, while the whitewashed walls prevent it from becoming overwhelming. The warm neutral hue of the terracotta floor further softens the look. The effect might not be as successful under greyer Northern skies, in which case a softer mid-blue, like that of the door opposite, is easier to live with. Blue and white is a classic colour palette that works well in any style of house.

If you opt for a palette of strong colours, temper them with plenty of neutrals or off-whites to keep the scheme easy to live with.

COLOUR HUNTING.

Be inspired by the sights of the coast when it comes to choosing a decorative scheme. Fishing boats, beach huts and painted doors and shutters all boast strong shades that weather to more manageable but still vibrant hues. Colour inspiration is everywhere: the bottom of this boat (above right) is painted red, white and blue, a combination that never fails. Tropical brights such as turquoise and aqua are another popular choice for coastal-inspired homes. If you opt for a palette of strong colours, temper them with neutrals or off-whites to keep the scheme easy to live with (opposite left).

DARK & HANDSOME

Dark colours are very on trend and there seems to be no end to their popularity when it comes to interior design. Don't just think of bright summer days by the beach; embrace stormy greys, blackened fishing huts, seaweedy greens and deep sea blues too. Rich and intense, these sombre shades can bring a sense of drama and depth to any scheme. Use them cleverly and you'll create a home with the wow factor. Again, it's all about creating a balance that you can live with; if you're worried about going too dark, try a feature wall or, if you choose to paint the whole room, keep furniture, flooring and accessories lighter. If you love the dark look, choose harmonious tones with shiny, reflective surfaces to bounce light around the room.

BOLD CONTRASTS.
The thundercloud grey of this wall is balanced by white woodwork and warmed up with a stripped wooden door (opposite). Try Little Greene for a great selection of greys and deeper-toned hues. Dark backdrops mixed with brighter accessories can create a very sophisticated look, reminiscent of Old Master paintings (this page).

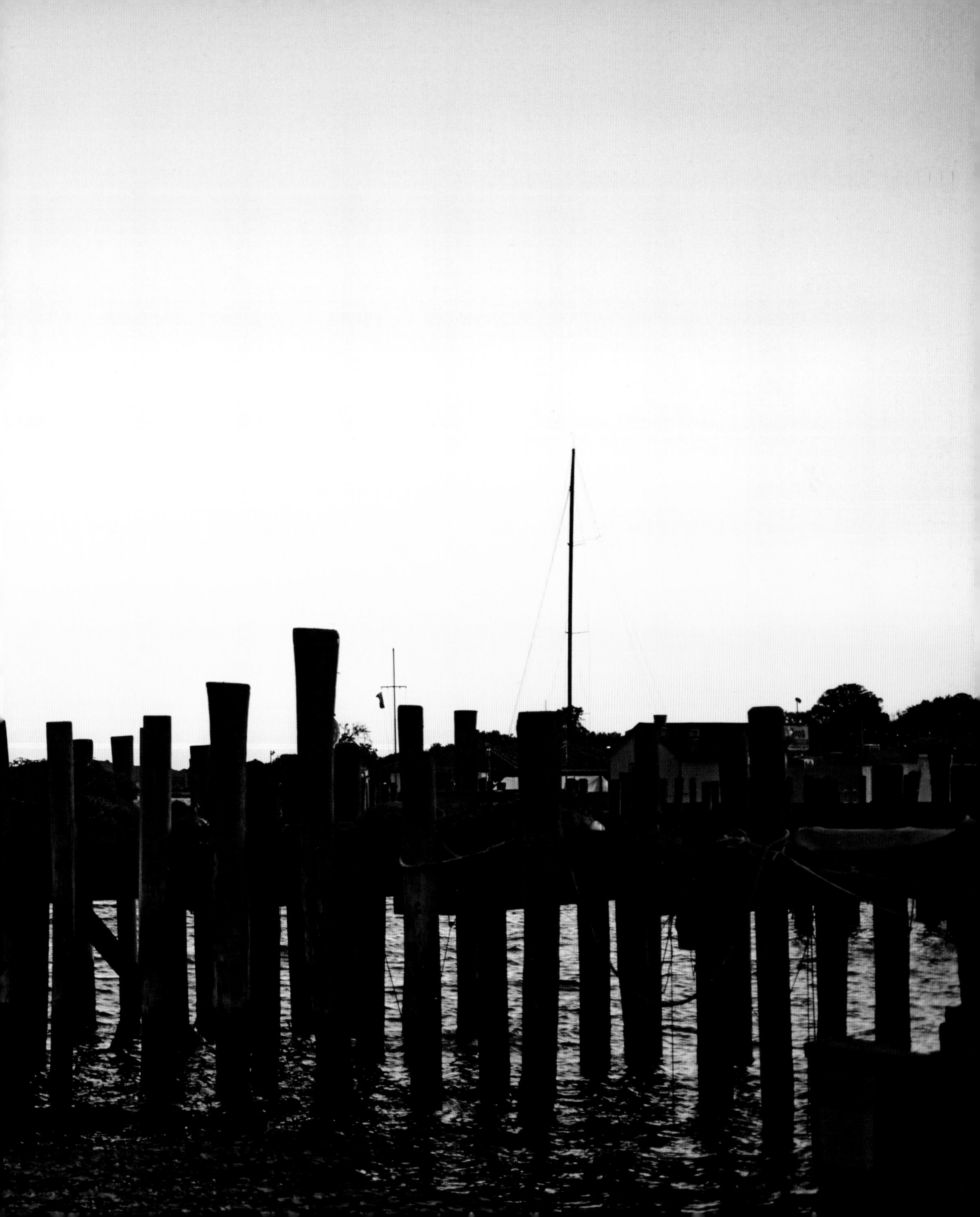

COASTAL *textures*

To me, a home without texture is a home without soul, so when it comes to decorating and styling interiors, seaside or otherwise, it's one of the most important elements to include.

WEATHERED, BLEACHED & FADED

Choosing textures and colours that are reminiscent of the sea shore will enable you to create an interior that evokes a soothing and relaxed vibe. Natural, bleached or distressed wood works well in coastal homes, as it brings to mind driftwood or other flotsam and jetsam shaped by the elements. The silvery hues and soft patina of worn wood is just right for a beach house, as are fabrics in tones that are slightly faded and seem to have been bleached by salt and sun. Loosely woven linens and sturdy cottons suggestive of sailcloth are perfect for providing texture. If you're sticking to a pale colour palette, contrasting textures add interest, depth and dimension.

WEATHERED AND WORN.
Sun-bleached whites and faded tones are easy to live with and will keep your home feeling light and bright (this page). Painted wood or shabby chic-style furniture works well in a coastal-inspired home (opposite). You can buy washed linen from Parna (in the UK) or Rough Linen (in the USA), and keep an eye out for peeling or distressed shutters at flea markets, antiques shops, salvage yards or on eBay.

STRIPPED & PAINTED WOOD

Look at any boatyard, harbour or row of beach huts and you can't help but be inspired by the beauty of wood that has been subjected to salty breezes and lashing waves. Whether you are drawn to the upturned hull of an old boat, flaking paint on the side of a beach hut or a sun-bleached wooden deck, all these effects can be recreated inside. Seek out furniture with a distressed or worn finish or pieces with a rich patina and aged look rather than anything too highly polished. When it comes to outdoor furniture, hunt down items with a bleached finish or those that have weathered to a silvery grey hue. New floorboards can be sanded back and treated with a light wax or Scandinavian lye soap for a simple coastal feel. For a utilitarian vibe, cover featureless walls with tongue-and-groove panelling or horizontal planking.

ROUGH IT UP.

Look out for original vintage pieces from flea markets, antiques fairs or car boot/yard sales, all of which are a good source of painted and distressed furniture and accessories. Chalk paint allows you to give furniture a rustic-style makeover without the need for prepping or priming. If you have a (not too precious) piece at home that doesn't have the right look, try ageing it yourself. Roughly sandpaper painted wooden items to reveal the grain of the wood beneath. Alternatively, place the piece of furniture outside and let it weather naturally (this works best for hardwoods such as teak and oak).

TEXTURAL LAYERING

Anything made of natural fibres, such as cotton, wool and linen or even hemp and hessian, will add the texture that is key to a coastal look, and loosely woven fabrics will always give a laid-back feel. Natural hues or the softer, sludgier colours created by organic dyes work well for a coastal-inspired home. Dress beds in vintage linen sheets, place striped linen grain sacks on the backs of chairs, use old sheets as a tablecloth or add a woollen throw to the end of your sofa. Old armchairs can be reupholstered in robust cotton or you can make loose covers/slipcovers from sturdy undyed linen for a more slouchy, relaxed effect. For a more wintery vibe, don't be afraid to use skins like sheepskins or faux fur for a really indulgent, cosy feel – they look warm and welcoming draped over sofas and will soften up hard chairs.

Sturdy cotton and linen can withstand salt water and the sun's harsh rays, while natural wool will keep you warm when the sun goes down.

HARDWORKING MATERIALS.

Textural fabrics are key to a relaxed, easy-going look and are a favourite element in my home. Antique linens can be found on eBay or from specialist dealers, while linen bedding (that fits modern beds), cushion covers and table linen are all available from companies such as Parna, Restoration Hardware and even H&M. For upholstery and soft furnishings, look at fine wool, simple lightweight voiles or practical striped cotton such as mattress ticking. Natural sheepskins are easy to find online and IKEA sell faux versions that can even be given a quick spin in the washing machine (opposite right).

NATURAL & WOVEN

WEAVING MAGIC.

As with linens and fabrics, don't be afraid to add lots of woven natural fibres to a scheme. When combined with plain sofas, white walls and simple patterned cushions, as in this low-key living area in a Spanish beach house (opposite), woven elements really help to add life and richness to a room. IKEA is a great place to look for attractive and affordable wicker furniture and accessories. If you don't want to invest in large pieces of furniture, opt for smaller items like lampshades and basketware that doubles up as extra storage. Vintage wicker and rattan furniture can be found at antiques fairs and reproduction pieces are also available.

Opt for woven furniture made from natural fibres such as wicker, rattan, rush or jute to bring interest to a seaside or coastal-inspired home. Rattan is a naturally sustainable climbing plant that grows abundantly in the tropics. After the canes are harvested, the outer skin is peeled away to be used as a weaving material and the core is cut into sections and steamed until it's soft enough to bend into shape for furniture. It's durable and lightweight with a strong core that makes it hard to break. Other natural fibres that work well are sisal, commonly used for making rope, twine and flooring, and coir, the fibre from the outer husk of the coconut, which is used for ropes, matting, doormats and mattresses. All natural fibres are versatile and hardwearing, and they work beautifully both indoors and out.

LIGHTING, FURNITURE
& windows

The decorative elements of a coastal home are key to a successful scheme. If you choose these items well, you'll have an interior that really looks and feels the part.

LIGHTING

Getting the lighting right is key to any interior design scheme and needs to be considered at the start of a renovation, especially if you are rewiring. The joy of a coastal-inspired theme is that you can choose from various different styles, from nautical-type fittings to enamel factory pendants – anything goes, as long as the colours work. Look for fittings in brass, copper or chrome, battered or weathered metal or delicate ceramics. Hanging pendants work well and can create a statement within a room, or opt for a lamp with a coloured or braided flex/cord. Natural copper will turn rich, mottled green over time, giving a beautiful patina to the metal.

ILLUMINATING OPTIONS.
A beautifully patinated funnel has been transformed into a pendant shade (above left); choose a hooked lamp holder hanging from jute-covered flex/cord or an industrial cage light for a retro, utilitarian vibe (above right and opposite); clip-on designs are versatile and practical (below left). Sturdy bulkhead lights originally designed for outdoor use and on ships look equally stylish inside (below right).

FURNITURE

When it comes to furniture, it's all about mixing and matching different styles and textures to create the relaxed, informal feel associated with coastal living. Mix rattan and wicker items with slouchy upholstered pieces and choose unfussy, utilitarian painted tables, shelving units and cabinets. Wicker furniture used to be synonymous with conservatories or sun rooms, but it can look just as good inside, softened up with lots of cushions and throws. It can even be painted – there are numerous tutorials on the internet. Other coastal-inspired styles are the famous Adirondack or Muskoka chair (above left), which is a simple slatted wooden chair generally used outdoors. Originally made from 11 wooden boards and featuring a straight back and seat with wide armrests, these make good companions for a relaxed coastal home.

TAKE A SEAT.
Choose distressed, weathered, vintage or painted furniture (this page and opposite). Home Barn Vintage has a good selection, as does Pottery Barn, and IKEA is also a great source of wicker furniture that will withstand the weather and look equally good indoors. Keep them comfortable by piling on cushions and throws.

WINDOW DRESSING

In a beach house, especially one only used during the summer months, you may find you don't need window treatments to keep out the cold. But if you are just attracted by coastal styling, it's a good idea to hang something at your windows for winter warmth, or even just for privacy. Keep window treatments fluid, soft and not too heavy. Avoid thick, interlined curtains, instead opting for lightweight voiles, lace and linens for a relaxed feel. Blinds/shades are a good solution, as they don't block out too much light. Roman and Swedish blinds pull up with a cord, allowing light to flood in while still allowing for privacy. They can be unlined too, ideal for softening a window without blocking any beautiful coastal light. Shutters are also a great solution – fuss free, simple and available in an array of colours.

HERE COMES THE SUN.
In a Spanish coastal home, a muslin/cheesecloth mosquito net filters the sun's rays. The wooden shutters keep out the fierce sun in the summer months and add a soft aqua accent to both the inside and outside of the house (above left and right). A delicate lace panel doubles as a curtain in a small bathroom (above centre), and a simple roll-up Swedish blind/shade has been fashioned from a length of loose-weave linen (opposite). If you are lucky enough to live in a warm climate, often only a sheer window treatment is necessary to provide a modicum of privacy without blocking out the light.

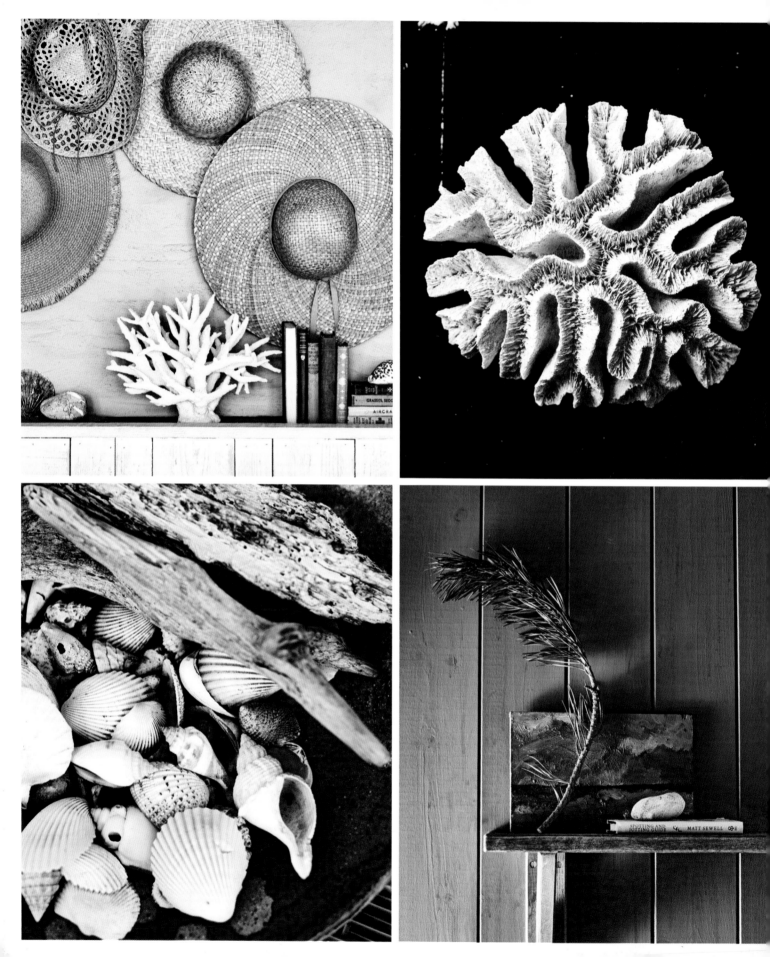

the art of DISPLAY

When it comes to display, don't be afraid to use items found by the coast. Washed-up shells, corals, driftwood and beach finds, displayed on their own or in a group, can look really effective.

BEACH FINDS & COASTAL TREASURES

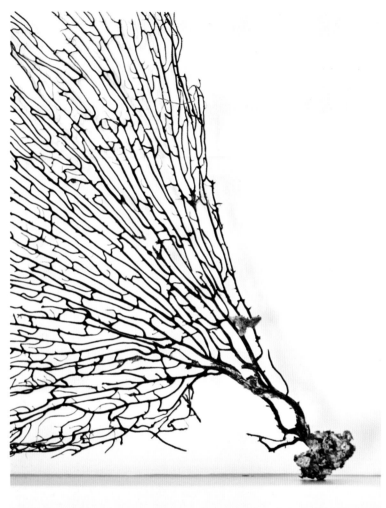

The sea washes up all manner of treasures, some of which are works of art in their own right. The chances are these items have been weathered, washed and battered by the waves and the elements, and are rich in texture and patina. Look out for pieces of driftwood as you walk along the shoreline – the early morning or low tide is the best time for beachcombing. It's also worth keeping an eye open for unusual items that will contribute to a beautiful textural still life – feathers, pieces of coral, shells or battered wooden buoys. Sometimes keeping it simple is key to the display, as it's the textures that make it interesting. Try to arrange things in clusters or groups of three – using items of different sizes and heights usually works well. Small items, such as sea glass or attractively coloured pebbles, look good piled up in glass jars.

Beachcombing often yields ocean treasures that make fascinating decorative features for a coastal or coastal-themed home.

NATURAL BEAUTIES.

Corals are beautiful intricate natural forms, but these days it's not advisable to buy anything that might have been harvested from already endangered reefs. Instead, choose from the vast array of faux coral designs – try Kelly Hoppen or Pottery Barn – that won't harm the coral reefs yet look as good as the real thing (above left and opposite left). Beach pebbles look charming arranged on a table top or mantelpiece or filling a glass jar (opposite right and above left), while a string of chunky weathered cork floats looks intriguing hanging from a peg rail (above right).

OCEAN TREASURES.
The beautiful natural forms of seashells and coral provide ample colour inspiration for a coastal home and can also be used as a decorative centrepiece. The sea often brings up chunks of coral or attractive shells that are no longer inhabited by any form of creature, but nowadays it's best to choose faux resin versions for a more environmentally friendly approach.

NAUTICALIA

Nauticalia is a phrase that encompasses all sorts of maritime memorabilia, including vintage nautical artefacts. Many such objects have been subjected to wind, salt and the relentless erosion of the waves, which in turn creates a desirable vintage look and a colour palette that's perfect for coastal or coastal-inspired homes. Look in ship's chandlers for nautical accessories or search coastal antiques shops or online for maritime antiques or nautical curios. Adding the right finishing touches will ensure that you create a soulful home reminiscent of life on and by the ocean. Getting the balance right is important though – you don't want to overdo it, or your home may resemble a beach-themed restaurant or fisherman's supply store.

RUGGED TEXTURES.
The texture and patina of old maritime equipment means it is often beautiful in its own right. A cork float hanging from a length of rope or a barnacled anchor (opposite), an old ship's compass, mooring or tow ropes and aged wooden buoys (this page) all make interesting and stylish decorative additions to any coastal or coastal-themed home. Other possibilities include old ships' bells, storm lanterns and navigational instruments (overleaf). Place such finds on walls, shelves or tables for dramatic effect.

VINTAGE MAPS & ARTWORKS

I love maps. I am drawn to their intricate beauty and detail, the information they impart and the way they use colour to indicate physical changes in elevation or depth. Vintage maps and navigation charts are even more appealing than their modern counterparts and are the perfect addition when it comes to decorating a coastal home. Inexpensive and easy to find online, you can frame old maps and hang them on the wall, pile stacks of them on a shelf, use an old globe that has been spun thousands of times as a table centrepiece or lay maps flat under a piece of toughened glass for a decorative tabletop. Anything will do, and any chart or map will look the part in your decorating scheme, simply because they are so beautiful.

GALLERY STYLE.

Scour local antiques shops in and around coastal towns for local maps or nautical charts that you can frame and hang as works of art in your home. There are many to be found on eBay or you could invest in a map or chart from somewhere like chartsales.co.uk, who are online stockists of thousands of genuine navigation charts.

COASTAL PLANTS

Plants and flowers bring any home to life, but in a coastal home, try decorating with plants or grasses that are indigenous to the local area rather than exotic specimens or blowsy flowers such as roses and peonies. Reeds and grasses, with their sculptural elegance, look wonderful simply placed in a large glass jar and left to fall naturally. Dried plants and seed heads, such as spiny-headed and prickly-stemmed teasels, have great architectural presence and intriguing forms. Succulents, such as sempervivums, offer striking arrangements of glossy green leaves, and are ideal plants for coastal homes, requiring little in the way of care.

VARIETY OF FORM.

Hardy grasses of any sort are ideal for coastal gardens, as they can withstand salt spray and harsh onshore winds (this page). They are elegant too, with their long feathery leaves, so look great when cut and brought inside (opposite). Teasels have intriguing spiny seed heads like giant thistles and are worth cutting and drying so that they can be displayed during the winter months. Succulents are perfect low-maintenance plants even for those of us who are less than green-fingered (below left).

coastal
HIDEAWAYS

EASY EATING.
In the dining room, John and Nicola fitted panelling to some walls to add interest and depth (left). The woodwork is painted Pavilion Gray by Farrow & Ball. Nicola chose oversized lighting to create a dramatic focal point over the dining table and mixed in rattan, wood and sheepskin to bring texture and softness to the look (opposite).

CORNISH *bolthole*

A Victorian cottage in the picture-postcard village of Port Isaac is a peaceful bolthole for interior designer Nicola O'Mara and her partner John Merriman.

Walking around Nicola and John's coastal retreat, the first thing that strikes you is the atmosphere of calm, thanks to a restful colour scheme inspired by the ocean. Nicola's use of natural materials such as slate, stone and wood add to the tranquil vibe, providing texture and interest wherever you look.

The couple describe their seaside home as a 'classic contemporary' Victorian house. It's located at the end of a narrow lane and, over the decades, quaint details such as an ornate wrought-iron balcony and gate had been added by previous owners, all of which contribute to the cottage's charm. As it's situated in a conservation area, Nicola and John were not able to make many changes to the exterior, apart from adding bifolding glazed doors to the kitchen area to allow more light to flood in. The interior, however, was a different story.

COMFY AND COSY.

The sitting room (above and previous pages) is snug, with a mixture of exposed stonework and wood-panelled walls and furniture gathered around a small but perfectly formed wood-burning stove that serves as a focal point during the colder months. Nicola covered the floor in a Moroccan-style rug and provided soft throws to snuggle beneath on chilly winter evenings.

When the couple bought the property, back in May 2014, it had been vacant for six years and was in need of some serious TLC. Located a stone's throw from the harbour and on a road out of the village, you can catch a glimpse of the sea from most of the windows and there's a glorious view from the terrace at the front. Port Isaac has been the location for films such as *Saving Grace* and *The Shell Seekers,* while the TV series Doc Martin is shot here. Despite this, the village remains almost untouched by development and has managed to retain its Cornish charm.

The renovation took two and a half years from start to finish. It was a huge project and included gutting the property, replumbing, damp-proofing, rewiring, reinforcing floors, reconfiguring the interior, constructing new walls and more. John carried out almost all the work himself, bringing in local contractors to help as and when necessary. In fact, John became something of a tourist attraction himself, as passers-by stopped to talk to him as he worked on the house. Many holidaymakers even popped back the following year to check on his progress!

Once the structural works were complete, the stone walls were repointed inside and out, and three new bathrooms and a kitchen were installed. Bespoke timber cladding was attached to the interior walls, bringing an extra dimension and depth to the space. When it came to a colour scheme, Nicola chose Farrow & Ball's Pavilion Gray for the

SHELL SEEKERS.

At one end of the kitchen, a vintage wooden printer's tray has been transformed into a stylish coastal display unit, holding shells gathered on trips to the beach. The rattan chairs are softened with sheepskins and plants bring life to the room, while the textured slate floor adds another layer of texture and visual interest.

HANGING AROUND.
A 1970s-style rattan hanging chair
has been suspended by the large
floor-to-ceiling window in the main
bedroom to make the most of the
wonderful sea views.

woodwork and Strong White for the walls. Soft furnishings are upholstered in complementary shades and the result is an interior that looks homely, welcoming and as if it has evolved over time. Nicola sourced much of the furniture from Scandinavian brands like Broste Copenhagen, House Doctor and Lene Bjerre. Some pieces are eBay finds, such as the dining room ceiling light, the wrought-iron shelves in the kitchen and the bench in the dining room.

The couple say that their favourite part of the house is the sitting room, where they like to relax with daughter Lola on the capacious sofa with the wood-burning stove roaring as the Cornish mists sweep in from the sea.

RELAXATION ZONES.
The main bedroom exudes pared-down luxury. The bubble pendant lights are from Danish brand House Doctor. Coastal elements such as shells and fan coral add a delicate touch to the scheme (above and right). Upstairs in the attic bedroom, John and Nicola left some of the original stonework exposed (far right). Sleek panelling and soft pink and grey soft furnishings contribute to the soothing atmosphere.

NEXT TO NATURE.
Both The Saltbox and The
Ferryman's are traditional
timber-framed shepherd's huts
on iron wheels. The Saltbox is
clad in cedar shingle tiles (this
page and opposite left) and
The Ferryman's in Siberian larch
planks, both chosen because
they will weather beautifully.

SHOWER WITH A VIEW.
On sunny days and warm, starry nights, guests can enjoy the outdoor showers – one of Georgina's favourite touches (above). Elmley is a family-run farm as well as a nature reserve, and the land is grazed by cows and sheep.

RURAL *retreats*

On the Isle of Sheppey, just off the Kent coast, Gareth and Georgina have created an unspoiled domain where visitors can leave the modern world far behind.

Looking out from The Saltbox and The Ferryman's at Elmley Nature Reserve, you would be forgiven for thinking you were on safari in the African Savanna rather than on the Isle of Sheppey in Kent. Georgina and Gareth Fulton and their young family – Barnaby, aged two, Eleni, three, and Polly the Springer Spaniel – have created two wonderful escapes that are a contemporary take on a streamlined modern cabin but with the cosy, rustic feel of a traditional shepherd's hut.

Sitting in the middle of a 3,200-acre nature reserve and family farm, the huts occupy a site of national and international significance. The surrounding water meadows and tidal marshes attract all manner of flora and fauna, including insects, hares, hedgehogs and water vole, along with a wide variety of birds. The coastal landscape gives huge skies and very special light. With uninterrupted views for miles, Elmley is a rare piece of wilderness only an hour from London.

MODERN RUSTIC.
The kitchen and headboard-cum-room divider at
The Saltbox are built from reclaimed wood from an
old forge, and the kitchen is fitted with a new wooden
worksurface and copper splashbacks that will age
beautifully (this page). For reclaimed wood and
planking, check out your local salvage yard or look
on eBay. LASSCO or Retrouvius are also good sources.

WARM AND SNUG.
The blankets and sofa throws add warmth and texture
(right and opposite). They are all from Romney Marsh
Wools, a local company that uses natural wool from
Romney sheep. The large bed cushions are the
Phragmite design by Francesca Baur for Fable & Base.

Both huts were built by Richard Lee at Plankbridge Ltd and transported from Dorset on a trailer.

Inside, the huts are fitted with comfy beds that look out through bifolding glazed doors onto seemingly never-ending views of wetlands and water. Oversized headboards divide the sleeping area from the pint-sized kitchenette and living area – a cosy, functional space with room for a child's bed – and a small but beautifully designed shower room.

The Saltbox, built in 2016, was named after the salt mounds that used to dot the marsh, as well as a nearby building where James II was held while under arrest in 1688. Both huts were built by Richard Lee at Plankbridge Ltd, who specializes in traditional shepherd's huts. For The Saltbox, the modern rustic style is at one with nature, with a nod to nearby industry and the rawness of the setting. As the interior is fairly neutral, it was important to add warmth with varying textures and paint colours. The main sleeping space is painted in Skimming Stone by Farrow & Ball, which complements the deep blue of Inchyra in the bathroom.

The focal point of The Saltbox interior is the rich hue of the reclaimed wood used for the headboard/divider and kitchenette, which was salvaged from an old forge in Bournemouth. This feature is matched with wall shelves fashioned from old scaffolding boards and utilitarian lighting from Tinsmiths. Enamel factory lights hang overhead, while the bedside reading lights are pared-down, simple brass fittings with bare oversized bulbs and fabric-covered flex/cord. In the kitchen, they opted for a durable copper splashback plus a copper shower head and industrial copper taps/faucets in the shower room. The finishing touches include a shower lined with corrugated metal and, just outside, a fire pit next to a couple of Adirondack chairs.

NATURAL MOTIFS.
The Ferryman's curtains feature Phragmite by Francesca Baur from Fable & Base printed on white voile and backed by a thicker fabric to keep the light out (opposite). The cushions are made from the same company's Bee Hive print, which is adorned with bold hexagons and tiny gold bees. Francesca made them in a bespoke colourway to tie in with the brass accessories (above) and green bathroom.

Francesca Baur, a textile artist at Fable & Base, created soft furnishings for both huts. Her designs are inspired by local flora and the bold Phragmite, based on a wetland grass, appears on the large bed cushions in The Saltbox and stands out against the distressed wood headboard. Other cushions feature her Sea Meadow print in a bespoke colourway of gentle blue-grey.

For the Ferryman's hut, Georgina and Gareth opted for a decor that is slightly more sleek and refined. The main space is painted in Farrow & Ball Slipper Satin with moody Green Smoke in the shower room. Again, the couple worked closely with Plankbridge on the interior, staining the wood of the kitchen and headboard to just the right shade using tea. Brass splashbacks in the kitchen and bathroom were distressed to give them a warm patina that's echoed in the Jim Lawrence antique brass Butler lights that hang over the bed and living area.

Elmley is an idyllic place to get away from it all – an unspoiled coastal escape with comfort and simple luxury thrown in for good measure.

A SENSE OF HISTORY.
Elmley has a fascinating agricultural and industrial history. The Ferryman's hut is so named due to its position near to the site of the old ferry over to the mainland, which became redundant when a bridge was constructed in the 1950s. In Victorian times, when someone wanted to cross over, they opened the door to the ferry hut to signal to the ferryman stationed on the other side to row over and get them.

DINING SPACES.
Dark grey weatherboarding and roof slates combined with Cornish stone walls bring a Scandinavian flavour to the exterior (left). The outdoor dining area offers an uninterrupted view across the fields to the sea (above). The open-plan dining area has muted tones, textured walls and wooden banquette seating for a casual, carefree vibe (opposite).

FAMILY *friendly*

A converted hayloft near St Mawes is the perfect spot for relaxed family living.

When James and Lisa Bligh bought their home on the south coast of Cornwall, it was what they describe as a typical holiday house with honey-coloured pine floorboards and jaunty striped nautical-style fabrics. The couple wanted to transform it into a more sophisticated, Scandinavian-inspired beach house and that is exactly what they did, giving the interior a complete makeover.

Working with a team of builders that they already knew, and despite an oil leak at the start of the project that prolonged the work by six months, Lisa and James managed to achieve a great deal in a relatively short space of time. New floors were laid throughout, a shower room was added, the bathrooms were updated and a wood-burning stove was installed in the living area.

The couple chose to update the existing kitchen, removing the wall cupboards and replacing them with open shelves, fitting a new worksurface and splashback, and repainting the units in Farrow & Ball's Down Pipe, a dark blueish-grey.

When it came to the decor, James and Lisa worked closely with Jess Clark, an interior designer at Unique Home Stays. They chose to limewash the wooden floor and ceiling beams and used a palette of muted greys on the walls, with Strong White by Farrow & Ball as one of the main colours. This creates a neutral backdrop, while the textured wood adds depth and interest to the scheme. The couple wanted to create a beachcomber, 'collected over time' feel, so the artwork and accessories are all vintage finds, including a seaplane propeller that now hangs on one of the bedroom walls. They introduced lots of varying textures in the form of loose-weave linens on the beds, sheepskins on the floor and unlined linen blinds/shades at the windows, creating an easy, lived-in feel. In a bid to encourage their four children to enjoy family time, in the sitting room the couple decided to conceal the TV behind a pair of vintage shutters complete with their original peeling paint.

The interior is full of rustic, relaxed charm. Vintage enamel pendant shades are suspended from jute-covered electric flexes/cords above the dining table and beds. In the window recesses, metal cleats secure the Swedish-style blinds/shades, while kitchen shelving hangs from nautical-style ropes. There are many ingenious display ideas too: a cluster of well-worn straw hats creates a textural art installation

above the dining area, and framed vintage nautical charts and maps cover the walls. Wooden model boats and winches nestle on shelves and coiled ropes hang on the stone walls, making reference to the house's location without sliding into coastal clichés.

The rough plaster walls of the hayloft were repainted and some areas were fitted with wooden cladding to add a contemporary element to the scheme. Lisa and James opted for second-hand and salvaged furniture where

MUTED HUES.
In the kitchen, James and Lisa chose a deep grey for the cabinets, and a soft geometric design for the tiled splashback with open shelving above to keep the space fuss-free (opposite). The limewashed wooden flooring that runs throughout the downstairs creates a sense of continuity and space (above). The couple employed the same effect on the ceiling beams for a modern touch.

EASY LIVING.
Touches of grey and black in the living space add interest and definition to the seating area (this page). The rattan table, slouchy sofa and tactile linen cushions create an easy-going feel, while unlined linen curtains allow light to flood in. The open-plan layout of the ground floor is relaxing and sociable – perfect for a coastal home (opposite).

THE SCILLY ISLES

It's only a short walk across the fields to unspoiled Pendower Beach, which is amazing for rock-pooling, and a short drive to St Mawes, an old fishing port.

possible, sourcing items from eBay and reclamation yards. The dining table base came from an old mill, an old chest doubles as a coffee table and a vintage locker has been put into service as a bedside table.

The open-plan living space leads out onto a patio and large deck, home to an outdoor eating area, and the garden is a safe haven for their four children, Max, Phoenix, Toby and Bonnie. The couple rent the field at the back of the house to a local farmer, so it's not unusual to have a herd of cows watching the family eat in the evening.

It's only a short walk across the fields to Pendower Beach, which is amazing for rock-pooling, and a short drive to St Mawes, an old fishing port now renowned for its sailing and restaurants. Unlike many coastal homes, this house is welcoming all year round. It works perfectly in the summer months, when it lends itself to open windows and cooling sea breezes, but is equally enticing during the winter, with the wood-burning stove at full blast.

A ROOM WITH A VIEW.

James and Lisa say that one of their favourite features of the whole renovation was the reconfiguration of the main bedroom. This allowed the couple to reposition their bed, which was previously tucked away under the eaves, to a spot that offers wonderful views across the fields and down to the sea. They agree that there is nothing better than lying in bed of a morning and surveying the scene (opposite). The whitewashed wooden cladding attached to the far wall adds texture to the room and creates a focal point within the scheme. Simple nautical accessories, richly woven fabrics and thick shaggy rugs all combine to create a cosy and welcoming master bedroom (this page).

THE ART OF DISPLAY.

Carefully curated coastal accessories strike the right note without looking contrived or overly styled (this page). In the spare room, propellers, corals and enamel pendant shades stand out against the soft grey walls, striped linens add visual interest and prints are hung from loops of nautical twine – an unsual detail.

OFF THE CHART.

Off-white tongue-and-groove panelling and painted textured walls create a calm backdrop (opposite). This bedroom is warmed up with an old wooden table and chair and a framed sailing chart on the wall. Both the bedroom and shower room have a Swedish blind/shade in loose-weave linen to allow maximum daylight.

PERFECTLY QUAINT.
The charming wooden seaside cottage was built in 1807 (right). Cape Cod is very important to the owners, as they have been summering here as a family for many years. The cosy, screened-in porch is a favourite spot (opposite). Vintage rattan furniture adds texture to the space, which has a soft grey painted floor and a yellow ceiling inspired by the kitchen.

CAPE COD *vintage*

This historic Cape Cod cottage has plenty of personality and vintage charm.

When Justine Hand and Chad Updyke bought Salt Timber Cottage in Rock Harbor on Cape Cod, they knew the property well. It was located just across the street from Justine's grandparents' house, and Justine, Chad and their children, Oliver, 12, and Solvi, 9, had rented the cottage for several summers. When the previous owner decided to sell, Justine was the obvious contender.

Dating back to 1807, the cottage was owned for many years by two sisters from Boston who had given it its last major remodel in the 1940s and Justine was keen to update it to what she describes as a 'not too cottagey cottage'. Most of the alterations were cosmetic – stripping old, dark wallpapers, taking down heavy curtains and painting some rooms in lighter, brighter shades.

The cheery yellow kitchen with its pitched roof was the only room left unchanged – the couple even retained the original stove. The family love to gather here around the table and it's one of Justine's favourite rooms.

The dining room sits at the centre of the cottage and has seven doors leading off it. It's a small space, so Justine found a local carpenter who used vintage pine boards to construct a narrow dining table with drop-leaf sections that can be folded down when necessary. The mismatched chairs that surround it are pulled together with several coats of Benjamin Moore's Linen White paint.

Along with the kitchen, other original features include the splatter-painted floors in the dining room and bedroom. These are typical of Cape Cod cottages and Justine points out that they are a wonderful way to add texture and interest to a room while hiding sand, dust and dirt.

When it came to the interior, Justine resisted the obvious beachy motifs, opting instead for the colours and textures of the coast. She has chosen utilitarian vintage pieces because their worn surfaces seem to fit well with the cottage and remind her of items washed up on the shore. The dining room, with its gently curved ceiling, is painted a soft, pale blue that Justine likens to the inside of a robin's egg. A small pantry leads off

MELLOW YELLOW.
The original yellow-painted kitchen is a focal point where the family enjoy spending time together, chatting, cooking and eating (this page and opposite). Justine left this room pretty much as it was, just touching up the paintwork as necessary. It's a simple, functional space with everything to hand – a well-used pan, chopping board and bread knife and onion basket hang from nails banged into the wall.

DOUBLE ASPECT.

The sitting room is comfortable, relaxed and flooded with light on both sides (this page). The pantry, just off the dining area, is one of Justine's favourite rooms, where she displays much-loved heirlooms (opposite left). The dining room, while something of a thoroughfare, is still a stylish and comfortable place to eat (opposite right).

When it came to the interior, Justine resisted the temptation to go for obvious beachy motifs, opting instead for the colours and textures of the coast.

this room and is lined with deep shelves that hold a collection of treasured tableware, including hand-shaped bisque vases and a black Wedgwood coffee pot that were handed down from Justine's grandmothers.

The soft blue shade continues into the living room, where Norwegian prints that once belonged to Justine's grandmother hang over an old Pottery Barn sofa with sturdy white cotton loose covers/slipcovers. The coffee table is an old workbench and the windows have been left bare, allowing the light to flow in.

Furnishings are comfortable and unpretentious, combining hand-me-down family pieces with cheerful but inexpensive accessories. The grey rug on the living room floor came from West Elm and replaced a seagrass rug that was just a little too quaint. Justine says that part of her job is to keep the cottage's charms in check and explains that the whole revamp has been something of an exercise in restraint.

The family's favourite hangout is the screened porch at the front of the house, which looks out towards the sea. This is where they relax after a day on the beach. The walls are painted in Benjamin Moore's Linen White with Stonington Gray on the floor, while the yellow-painted ceiling was inspired by the soft hue of the kitchen walls.

PERFECTLY IMPERFECT.
The main attic bedroom is calm, serene and filled with light. Justine has furnished it with rush matting, simple furniture and a few carefully chosen accessories (this page).

STATEMENT ART.
At the top of the staircase that leads up from the dining room to the attic bedroom, a vintage nautical chart of Cape Cod Bay takes centre stage. The knotty beams and old tongue-and-groove walls up here are painted in a creamy white shade that just seems to get better with age (this page and opposite).

The guest bedroom has a green splatter-painted floor and original 1940s wallpaper. Justine found the iron bed frame on eBay and the tab-topped curtains came from IKEA. Stairs off the dining room lead up to the master bedroom, tucked away under the eaves. Justine kept the walls pale here to make the most of the light and chose soft, washed linens for a cosy, inviting effect. The ship's lantern hanging from the ceiling came with the cottage.

You can't help but feel at peace here, surrounded by the gentle colours and simple furnishings that Justine has used to create a wonderfully understated coastal home.

DAINTY DESIGN.
Justine left the original 1940s wallpaper in the guest room exactly as it was when they moved in (opposite). Other favourite pieces in this room include the old wrought-iron bedstead, bedside table and vintage lace and linen bedding. The compact bathroom is home to more delicate vintage wallpaper, tongue-and-groove panelling and muted blue-grey tones, which give a coastal feel to the room without being clichéd (above).

UNDER THE EAVES.
A small dormer window in the attic bedroom reveals the beams and timber framework of the old cottage. Sun hats are hung casually from nails banged into the eaves (right).

ON THE *waterfront*

A Long Island beachfront cottage with bags of quirky vintage charm.

Elena Colombo describes the waterside cottage that she shares with partner Lavelle and Rosie the black Labrador as 'eclectic', and when you enter you can see why. It's the combination of wood-clad walls, wooden floors and mix-and-match colours and fabrics, teamed with lots of personal elements that she has amassed over the years. Elena started renting the property in 1994 and bought it when it came up for sale in 1999. The cottage sits at the East End of Long Island near Greenport, a historical whaling and shipbuilding port situated at the entrance to Peconic Bay.

During Elena's tenure, the century-old house has undergone two renovations, the most recent in 2015–17 when the kitchen and porch were updated. She cheerfully admits, however, that maintaining the cabin is an ongoing project, one that she manages with lots of help from her contractors, Jared and Tibor of Vector East.

BRIGHT OUTLOOK.
The view from the back of Elena's cottage looking out over the Peconic River (this page). Her newly renovated kitchen with its Windsor chairs, painted woodwork, pops of bright colour and her collection of oyster plates (opposite).

COASTAL CONTRASTS.
Elena chose a palette of soft coastal-inspired colours from Farrow & Ball for the interior (above and opposite).
The mid-century day bed was left by the previous owners, and Elena reupholstered the seat cushion with
deckchair stripes and adorned it with cushions in contrasting and complementary coastal prints (above).

One of the first major jobs she undertook after buying the cottage was reroofing the structure, which was done using traditional red cedar shingles. Then the rotting windows were replaced with vinyl-clad, double-glazed timber versions. The next big renovation took place in 2012, after Hurricane Sandy swamped the building, resulting in a new, more 'grown-up' kitchen.

Elena admits to being a lover of colour. Originally, her beloved kitchen was daffodil yellow with lots of red enamel pots by Dansk and Le Creuset. When the room was redecorated last year, she installed a cornice/crown molding that she painted in Mole's Breath by Farrow & Ball – a sober warm grey hue. Elena says the detailing reminds her of a Puritan lighthouse or a New England museum. The living room walls are a tranquil bluey grey that she tried to match to one of those overcast days where the water and sky seem to blend into one. Her style is to keep the backdrop soft and neutral, and to add bursts of colour via accessories, throws and cushions in red, orange and hot pink to keep the feel upbeat.

MIX AND MATCH.

Elena likes to add bits and pieces to her coastal home as and when she sees them, recently buying a vibrant Indian Kantha bedspread with splashes of magenta for the bedroom (opposite and below). This works well against the light tonal colours on the walls and ceiling, and picks up the rich hues of the threadbare rug on the floor.

VINTAGE THING.

The tiny bathroom is painted in a palette of stormy greys with an original galvanized bathtub that fits neatly at the end of the space. Elena's precious collection of boat paintings are propped up on the wooden framing of the walls (right).

When it comes to furniture, Elena explains that she loves the simplicity of mid-century style, but generally she buys things she likes with little or no planning, which adds to the eclectic look of the interior. The large day bed in the living room area was in the house when she moved in and works well in combination with the cosy cottage style she's drawn to.

Elena has a love of lighting and lamps, with a stylish selection dotted around the cottage. 'I'm a lighting fanatic, especially lamps. I love everything about them – they are not only hugely practical but they also act as jewellery for your room.' When it came to the soft furnishings, she started out with a loosely nautical theme that

included French stripes, linens, coral and seashell prints, but recently she has added some Indian prints in the form of bedding.

One of Elena's favourite features is the display of boat paintings in the bathroom. Sourced from yard sales and antiques stores, she has chosen the same style frame for all the pictures to tie the look together. Elena also loves the traditional mortise and tenon bookshelf to the left of the fireplace, which she designed with her friend, local craftsman Dave Nyce. This houses books found at the local dump, which has a reuse centre where people can drop off unwanted items and pick up new finds at the same time.

It's evident that there is a lot of love and happiness in this home. Elena's company, Fire Features, designs and makes fire pits, and she has installed a fire bowl by the water's edge. It was the first piece she designed for her propane gas fire pit collection and it has become a focal point for friends and family, somewhere to gather together by the water.

SUNSHINE AND SHOWERS.
One of the most charming features of Elena's home is the outdoor shower that she had fitted at the side of the house. Both pretty and practical, it's a great place to cool down at the end of a long day in the sun or rinse off sandy, salty limbs after a trip to the beach. Elena has decorated it with a dried mushroom coral and a curtain of shells knotted onto string (this page).

FIERY FOCAL POINT.
At the back of the cottage, by the water's edge, Elena has installed one of her own propane gas-fuelled fire pits. It acts as a focal point and is surrounded by a variety of seating piled with cushions for added comfort.

COASTAL
simplicity

Bringing this shingled cottage up to date was a labour of love for designer Hannah Childs.

It was the entrance hall that inspired the renovation of this rambling seaside cottage on Long Island Sound. When the owners bought it, towards the end of 2012, much of the house had been 'winterized' to make it suitable to live in all year round, and as a result the interior was dark, dank and mouldy. However, the exposed timber-framed walls, original sash windows and wooden floors of the entryway made them believe they could recreate the same look throughout.

SOMEWHERE TO RELAX.
The exterior of this coastal home is clad in cedar shingles that are typical of the local area and will gradually weather to a beautiful silvery grey. The verandah was extended in the rebuild and is the perfect place to relax and unwind (right).

Having spent a great deal of time in the area during her childhood, the new owner and her family had relocated to San Francisco. She sought professional help from old friends – local architects Allee Architecture and interior designer Hannah Childs – who both assured her that they could restore the spirit of the original house. Not only that, but they also promised that the renovation would be completed by the beginning of the next summer (and it was).

As was typical of late-19th-century cottage construction of the area, the house had been built without foundations, so was sitting directly on dirt and slowly rotting away. It was decided to raise the structure by 1.8m/6ft to lay a reinforced concrete foundation. The house was lifted and lowered back onto the new foundation, and two dehumidifiers were installed to draw out moisture. Passers-by were amazed by the huge effort involved in saving the original structure, but having done so, the owners feel they have preserved a valuable piece of history for the local community.

WHITE AND BRIGHT.
The kitchen is a mix of handmade cabinets and open shelving crafted from the original floorboards of the house (above and left). The central island provides additional storage and work space, and the enamel shades and bold striped rug add interest to the scheme. White tableware keeps the look fuss free (left). The boxed-in main staircase utilizes a sturdy old mooring rope in place of a handrail (far left and opposite).

The success of the redesign lies in the bright, light and airy feeling that suffuses the interior. There's no clutter or fuss.

WELCOME HOME.
It was the hallway that inspired the purchase of the cottage (above). The owner loved the exposed wooden framing and used it as the basis for the renovation. In the homey living room, a custom-made chunky sisal rug sits on top of reclaimed wood flooring (opposite).

Many original local houses had been renovated or torn down, so this was a particularly worthy project for interior decorator Hannah Childs, who describes her work on the house as a 'labour of love'. The owners wanted the refurbished house to feel lived in, with a relaxed mix of old and new. In the bright and airy cottage kitchen, Hannah repurposed some of the original chestnut floorboards as kitchen shelves. Local carpenter Steve Dunn handcrafted the cabinetry, bar and kitchen island top, even placing a 2013 penny in the island and sealing it with resin. Upstairs, the pine floors were sanded down and covered in a clear finish to bring out the warm tones of the wood.

When it came to the decorative scheme, the owner was insistent that she wanted little or no colour. The downstairs rooms flow into one another and it was easy to agree on softly shaded White Dove by Benjamin Moore for the walls and ceilings. The kitchen stairs are a quirky feature, with a painted blue stripe reminiscent of vintage French linen running down the centre and a copper-pipe handrail. Neutral linens were chosen for the sofa and armchairs, with touches of subtle blues and greens in the shape of cushions and throws. The furniture is understated. Wooden pieces add warmth, while white metal Tolix chairs are paired with a battered old farm table in the kitchen.

The exterior of the house needed to blend in with neighbouring buildings, so Hannah chose traditional nautical-style outdoor lighting from Urban Archaeology. The interior lighting is a mix

THE LIVING IS EASY.
The cottage windows are hung with woven blackout blinds/ shades that block the sun's rays (opposite). In the dining room, the Mandala rug came from Madeline Weinrib and the white oak dining room table was designed by Allee Architecture and built by Alfred Brown Cabinetry in Warren, Connecticut (this page and left). The Serena & Lily lampshades add texture to the scheme.

of wooden lamps and modern fittings with reclaimed green factory pendants over the island unit in the kitchen. Exterior walls were covered in white cedar shingles typical of New England coastal architecture, which, as they weather, will turn an attractive silvery grey shade.

The success of the redesign lies in the bright, light and airy feeling that suffuses the interior. There's no clutter and fuss, nothing is over-thought or over-styled and the atmosphere is one of simple comfort. Hannah readily admits that the project was particularly meaningful to her. She was the main point of contact for the architect and subcontractors, and installed everything from the furniture to the gallery of photos upstairs and even the kitchen accessories. 'I remember the evening I left the house ready for [the owners'] arrival from California – I felt as if I was leaving a part of me. It was such a reward to see them the following day, after their first night in this house they had looked forward to for so long.'

SUBTLE STRIPES.

Vintage linens were the inspiration for the painted staircase that leads off the kitchen and the handrail was crafted from a length of old copper piping (above right). The bedrooms are calming havens of soft pastel blues, greys and greens, with woven fabrics contributing textural interest (above and opposite). The walls throughout are whitewashed to keep the look cohesive and to show off the internal framing of the walls.

BATHING BEAUTY.

A rug from Dash & Albert keeps the wooden floor in the bathroom dry, while a traditional-style basin and tub work perfectly alongside the industrial aesthetic of the Back Bay wall lights from Urban Archaeology (right).

relaxing
BAY RETREAT

BESIDE THE SEASIDE.
The compact beachfront cottage had been remodelled over the years, but a complete renovation was necessary after the building was devastated by Hurricane Sandy in 2012. It now sits proudly on the beach, with a flight of steps leading down onto the sand and a raised terrace that's the perfect spot for watching the world go by (above and opposite).

This beachfront cottage on the North Fork of Long Island epitomizes relaxed coastal living.

Richard and JoAnn Savarese's beach retreat on Long Island is serene, white, bright and super-relaxed. Fondly named LaDiDa, the cottage is situated on the peaceful, rural North Fork. Originally this was a small community of fishermen and farmers, but from the early 1900s it developed into a popular destination for families eager to escape the oppressive summer heat of New York City. Many of those families still own homes in the area.

LaDiDa was originally a fishing cabin, built at the beginning of the 20th century and measuring only 4.5 x 4.5m/15 x 15ft. It was evidently constructed from whatever repurposed materials were to hand at the time, including cedar planks, old window frames and a door jamb that was once a roof rafter and which is still intact. At some point in the 1930s, the cabin was transported by barge from remote Orient Point, at the very far end of the North Fork, to its current location. At various intervals after that, previous owners built onto the wooden structure, increasing its size to 49sq. m/528sq. ft – the footprint that remains today.

A SENSE OF CALM.
The living area has tall windows and sliding doors that overlook the raised terrace area and the bay beyond (opposite). The wooden coffee table was a junk-shop find that was repainted to match the scheme. The newly fitted kitchen is compact and functional, combining simple white units with pale, grey-green tiles and a dark worksurface that is sleek and robust (left).

When Richard and JoAnn became empty nesters, they decided to downsize from a larger holiday house. They fell in love with LaDiDa as soon as they saw it and they purchased the cottage in September 2001. The couple enjoyed holidays there for many years without making any changes, simply delighting in the relaxed tempo of beach life. However, in October 2012 the cottage was severely damaged by Hurricane Sandy. The force of the storm knocked the building off its foundations, leaving it sinking into the sand. JoAnn and Richard faced a difficult decision – to knock the cottage down and start again, or to restore and renovate. They chose the latter.

The restoration began in 2014 with the raising of the house and the pouring of a new concrete foundation. A new aluminium roof was added and the exterior was clad in sturdy shiplap siding. Inside, all the plumbing and electrics were replaced and new windows, doors and floors were fitted. Glass sliding doors were installed to give access to the raised terrace and replace a small wooden door that blocked the view. The couple took the opportunity to fit a new kitchen, choosing white cabinets and a quartz worksurface, as well as a new bathroom with underfloor heating, walk-in shower and a new tub.

The central living space consists of a seating area and dining nook that boasts banquette seating with ample storage space beneath the seats. White-painted rattan furniture keeps the space light and bright, while the coffee table was a lucky find at a local church flea market and was whitewashed to cover the original dark wood. The couple chose pale grey paint for the walls and

whitewashed the cedar floorboards. The cottage is home to an array of coastal ephemera: books, corals and shells found locally, along with paintings by local Peconic Bay Impressionist artists, all of which help to bring a tranquil seaside vibe to the compact interior.

Throughout the remodelling, JoAnn and Richard collaborated with their daughter Marissa, an interior designer, who helped them choose design details, colour schemes and materials, as well as keeping the project on track. Other key members of the team included architect Mark Schwartz, Tom Sanders of Custom Carpentry and stonemason Julio Nunez, who all worked together to obtain the necessary permits to restore the historic property.

Once the project was finished, the couple bought a 1966 Airstream to offer additional guest space and add to the relaxed vibe of the house. They plan to enjoy the beautifully renovated cottage to the full, sharing it with family and friends and watching the moon rising over the lighthouse from the deck.

A COSY CORNER.
The open-plan living space is home to a snug corner dining area tucked under the sloping roof. JoAnn and Richard's contractor constructed the L-shaped banquette seating, which conceals lots of practical storage space under the seats (opposite). The walls in this space are clad in whitewashed horizontal boarding, providing a tranquil backdrop for the paintings, books and coastal souvenirs that the couple have collected over the years (above left). The collection of vintage *Yachting* magazines (above right) came from the White Flower Farmhouse homeware store in nearby Southold (see pages 120–127). The fabrics chosen for the dining area are simple and understated, with small delicate patterns and subtle stripes (below left and right).

DREAM MACHINE.

The Savareses' original 1960s Airstream trailer is parked alongside LaDiDa and doubles as overflow accommodation when guests come to stay (left). The cottage overlooks Long Island Sound (above and opposite). This was once a sleepy community of fishermen and farmers, but about a hundred years ago the area started to become a popular holiday destination for families escaping the summer heat of New York City. Some of the houses on the estate have remained unchanged since those early days, adding to the quaint charm of the surroundings.

Located on the quiet, low-profile North Fork of Long Island, JoAnn and Richard's cottage sits on one of the many pristine beaches of Long Island Sound.

WOOD AND WHITES.
The dining space at one end of the kitchen is a stylish mix of simple, functional furniture, rustic shelves and wooden beams (opposite and left). The mix of whites creates a calm elegance. The exterior is typical of local architecture, with a deep covered porch (above and below left).

SEASIDE *salvage*

The renovation of Lori and Stephen's 19th-century farmhouse on Long Island involved lots of salvage, surprises and simple coastal styling.

The quaint seaside village of Greenport on Long Island's North Fork was originally settled in the late 17th century. Here, just a short walk from the harbour, beach and town centre, Lori Guyer and husband Stephen have created their dream home in their ideal location. Lori, owner of the White Flower Farmhouse homeware store in Southold, lives there with Stephen and children Colin, 23, and Shannon, 21, as well as Otto the Miniature Schnauzer.

The farmhouse, originally built in 1868, was bought by the couple in 2013, but they didn't move in until spring 2014, after a 14-month renovation carried out by Stephen Owen of Red Barn Woodworking in Eastport. Lori describes the renovation as a process of uncovering the hidden beauty of the building, literally peeling back the layers to let the beautiful bones of the house emerge.

FARMHOUSE STYLE.
The white-painted kitchen is accessorized with stainless steel and worn woods. Industrial pendant lights add interest at ceiling height (this page). Clever display areas are a hallmark of this coastal home (above). A merchant's style dresser/hutch houses dining essentials and Lori designed shelving to go above it (opposite). Here, she displays her white china, vintage finds and glassware.

During the work they uncovered many surprises, including a dirt floor in the basement made with stones from a ship's ballast. Under the floor of another room was an open stack-stone well that had just been covered over without filling it in. The existing stone foundations of the farmhouse had to be reinforced and a new concrete foundation was poured to add strength. The contractors then began to strip away the layers. Once they started opening up the walls, builder Stephen decided to save anything that might come in useful.

He erected a huge tent complete with racks to hold old floorboards and beams as they were removed.

Outside, new cedar clapboard siding was fitted over a damp-proof membrane and the windows were trimmed, glued, screwed together, primed and painted before installation. After all the windows had been fitted and the house was watertight, they embarked on the task of putting the interior back together again, using salvaged and vintage elements wherever possible in an attempt to be faithful to the house's past and its surroundings.

Upstairs, the ceilings were removed to expose the original beams, which were then restored, and the original staircase and handrail were repaired to retain the original carved detailing. For the kitchen, the couple chose custom-built cabinets and a pantry in a traditional farmhouse style. In the downstairs bathroom, salvaged pieces were used wherever possible, and the original attic staircase in the master bedroom was left bare, displaying the original lath and plaster. Lori is proud of the fact that they were able to salvage a great deal of wood during the renovation and then to reuse it to line walls and to make cabinets, shelving and even a mantelpiece.

When it came to the finishing touches, Lori added a curated assortment of her own personal treasures alongside a selection of natural elements such as shells, beach glass and driftwood as well as nautical pieces found locally.

For the interior, Lori chose a simple, rustic style, mixing natural pine, industrial metal and white-painted furniture for texture and warmth. Her favourite feature is the old pine floor that was

DECORATING MASTERCLASS. The dining room and living room are a lesson in how to use contrasting textures to enliven an all-white scheme (this page and opposite). Lori has combined timber cladding on the walls with wide, bleached floorboards, cotton curtains and rush mats. A wooden dining table and armoire contribute warm tones, while the dull lustre of industrial-style metal chairs, a folding table and a trolley adds depth. Unexpected nautical details bring the room to life (right and far right).

discovered during the renovation – some of the planks are 53cm/21in wide – and her best-loved piece of furniture is the kitchen table; an old German butcher's table found in a flea market. Fabrics are mostly relaxed, textured whites and linens, and the Restoration Hardware sofas have practical loose covers/slipcovers making them easy to care for. Many things were found at local yard sales, flea markets and vintage shops. The majority of the lighting came from Barn Light Electric and other industrial and nautical lights were sourced on eBay. But what really shines out here are the personal touches throughout this stylishly simple coastal abode, making it a home with soul.

DESIGN DEVICES.
The bedrooms are full of inspiring ideas and clever tricks (this page and opposite). Opening up the ceiling revealed the original beams in the main bedroom and a mooring rope was used to hang a ceramic French style pendant light above the bed (far left). White linens, cottons and throws soften these spaces, while extra texture is added in the form of rush baskets, weathered wood and a rattan chest (opposite).

For the interior, Lori chose a simple, rustic style, mixing natural pine, industrial metal and white-painted furniture for texture and warmth.

the coastguard's HOUSE

INDIVIDUAL APPROACH.
The bare floorboards in the hallway add warmth to white woodwork and pale walls. Much of the furniture is vintage and was sourced from Ardingly Antiques market. Quirky accessories such as the wooden decoy duck add personality to the space (above). The open-plan dining area is an eclectic mix of Shaker, mid-century and industrial elements (above right and opposite).

Owners Jane and Martin swapped city streets for a new life in the historic port of Deal.

Despite being charmed by the ancient Cinque Port town of Deal on the Kent coast when visiting friends, Martin and Jane Will never thought they would end up living there themselves. However, they relocated from London in 2012 and have since created a welcoming coastal abode for themselves and their Highland Terrier Baxter.

The Wills' detached Victorian house was built in 1860 for the town's Head Coastguard and stands proudly on the seafront in the centre of Deal. Behind it is a row of cottages that were built at the same time for the brave coastguards and their families. Today, the new coastguard lookout station is right next door, and as Martin is a member of the local search and rescue service, his commute to work is very quick indeed!

Renovating the house has been something of a labour of love for the couple, and although they've achieved a great deal, Martin says there's still more to do. They began by tackling the structural work, employing a builder to knock down the wall between the kitchen and dining room. Martin and Jane toyed with the idea of a

custom-built designer kitchen, but instead decided to employ Martin's brother, who is a carpenter, to make and install one instead. They painted the cabinets in Railings by Farrow & Ball, fitted white metro tiles and painted the walls white to keep the look fresh and simple. The zinc-topped dining table is surrounded with an array of mid-century and Shaker-style dining chairs, and pieces of art adorn the walls, many of them by local artist Caroline Yates.

One essential job was refurbishing the damaged windows at the front of the house and replacing those at the side that had rotted due to exposure to the elements. Shutters were installed in the living area and bedrooms, along with a log burner downstairs. The couple undertook the rest of the refurbishment themselves: Martin panelled the study and fitted tongue-and-groove cladding to various walls in the house to create a cosy, utilitarian feel that seems appropriate for an old coastguard's house.

When it came to the decor, the couple opted for colours that were in keeping with the surroundings – soft greys and inky blues from Farrow & Ball. The muted tones give the interior a restful, timeless feel, especially as they are teamed with simple, functional pieces of furniture, bare wooden boards and vintage nautical items displayed all around the house. Fabric choices include washed linen, French striped fabrics, blue and white ticking and faded cottons, some of which

IN THE MIX.
The kitchen is the central hub of the open-plan ground floor (above). The deep blue cabinets and white metro tiles create a contemporary vibe, with the old floorboards adding a rustic touch. The living area is snug and cosy, with a deep, slouchy sofa and brown leather armchair (opposite). Lots of the vintage pieces, such as this pestle and mortar, were found by the couple while on buying trips for Will & Yates, their store in the centre of Deal (right).

When it came to the decor, the couple opted for colours that were in keeping with the surroundings – soft greys and inky blues from Farrow & Ball.

were sourced from Ardingly Antiques market in West Sussex. Jane and Martin are always in search of interesting wares for their gallery and store Will & Yates, which in turn means that the house is peppered with intriguing finds.

At the back of the house, there is a small courtyard that's something of a sun trap. Martin renovated the space in time for a birthday party one year, constructing raised beds and planting acanthus and olive trees in vintage washtubs. For the landscaping, he laid a mixture of slabs and decking – the perfect combination for a seaside house – and this, plus the mix-and-match furniture, keeps the look laid-back and informal.

Jane and Martin admit that the house is something of an ongoing project – next they plan to tackle the bathrooms and the front garden. In the meantime, it's a place where they can kick back and relax. Jane describes how much she loves the view from their bed – the shutters at the window open to reveal an uninterrupted panorama of sea and the sky. When you glimpse a view like that, it's all too easy to understand why Jane and Martin swapped the bright lights of the city for the big skies of the coast.

TIME FOR BED.
Jane and Martin have kept the bedrooms simple and soothing, mixing white walls with grey tongue-and-groove panelling on the walls (above). Cheerful striped cottons and textured linens contribute to the laid-back vibe, with a touch of warmth added in the form of an old wooden bedside table. The graphic bedside lamp base was made from an old wooden buoy.

CALMING PALETTE.

Sticking to a simple, harmonious colour palette gives the interior a sense of cohesion. Jane and Martin have combined mellow wooden tones with cool whites, deep blues and stormy greys (above). The result is an understated atmosphere that's perfectly in keeping with the coastal setting without being clichéd.

ON DISPLAY.

An old painted peg shelf on the bathroom wall is both practical and decorative – the perfect place to display nautical touches and favourite beach finds (right). The rustic wooden bath-caddy has a weathered texture that's reminiscent of driftwood (above right).

The front door opens straight into the kitchen area and hall (opposite), which lead, in turn, directly into the living space. Quirky treasures have been amassed over the years, creating an easy-going, eclectic vibe (this page). A nautical chart of the area hangs close to the entrance (above).

NORFOLK *beach shack*

A secluded coastal abode in deepest Norfolk offers a welcome escape from the big smoke for Sian and Stuart Boreman and their family.

Sian and Stuart Boreman describe their coastal bolthole on the Norfolk coast as somewhere that's naturally evolved over the years with no grand plan behind it. But what is evident upon entering The Shack is that, whether intentionally or not, the couple have created a welcoming, laid-back home that makes you feel relaxed from the moment you walk in.

The wooden cabin was constructed in the 1930s and refurbished in the 1960s, and is one of just two remaining buildings built as holiday homes just before the Second World War. At the time, there were plans for a whole holiday camp to be developed, but this never came to pass and instead The Shack sits in a tranquil spot in the middle of a field. It's just a short walk across farmland to a quiet and secluded sandy beach, which is one reason why the Boremans love it so much.

EASY OPEN-PLAN LIVING.
Basic elements, such as the plywood ceiling and the tongue-and-groove cladding on the walls, combine to create a warm and textured space. Industrial and mid-century elements blend seamlessly together. The wood burner is a focal point and warms the whole house.

The furnishings are an eclectic mix sourced from local auctions, eBay and local car boot/yard sales.

The couple, along with their two daughters Isabella and Iris, hankered after a place near the sea to escape from London. Having spent many weekends searching the Suffolk and Norfolk coasts, they happened across The Shack. It was raining and the kids were crying. 'It was the last estate agent and we thought about not bothering,' Sian explains. 'I went in and the agent said "I have this house, but you won't be interested, it has no water or electricity and it's very isolated." Perfect, I thought!'

The basic structure of the cabin has not changed, but the couple have rejigged much of the interior since they bought it 17 years ago, and work has been ongoing ever since. At the start, there was no mains water supply or electricity connection. However, by coincidence, Sian had been working with a photographer in London who was from the area and his brother, a local farmer, helped dig the trench for the water pipe. Other renovations included ripping up the pink flowery carpets and covering the walls with tongue-and-groove cladding. Initially, the couple decided to paint the existing mock Tudor beams, but eventually they removed the whole ceiling, taking it up to full roof height, which created a great sense of space. Stuart and a friend spent a weekend painting the fireplace, complete with its old gas fire, but they subsequently realized they should have just knocked the whole thing down, which they did the following weekend. The fire was replaced with a log-burning stove that comes into its own at night as a focal point within the room.

The furnishings are an eclectic mix sourced from local auctions, eBay and local car boot/yard sales. They're a blend of mid-century and industrial pieces, combining Ercol day

BACK TO BASICS.
The kitchen is basic and functional, combining open shelving with a retro cooker and enamel cooking utensils that fit perfectly with the look (above). The dining area houses Stuart's vintage speakers and sound system, and looks over the fields to the sea beyond. Ercol chairs sit opposite an old bench and a bright blue stool adds a splash of colour (opposite). A vintage map hangs on the wall (top).

CABIN HAVEN.
The main bedroom is a haven of comfort and laid-back style with many worn elements such as an antique iron bedstead, a wooden fruit-picker's ladder and bare floorboards. The distressed wooden shelving unit is filled with a collection of pocket-sized Observer's guides (this page and opposite below left).

beds with factory-style pendant lighting and framed nautical charts with 1960s ceramics. The interior walls are white, teamed with vintage fabrics in washed-out colours and the occasional pop of colour. Nothing in the house is so precious that they have to worry about it. This mix-and-match decorating style has resulted in a relaxed vibe that's perfect for a coastal home.

Sian and Stuart say that the verandah they had built on the back of the house is probably the best addition. It's where they sit on long summer evenings to watch the sun go down behind a nearby lighthouse. Their future plans for the cabin include replacing the uPVC windows with metal-framed Crittal versions and possibly adding a new tin roof.

Most importantly, time spent at The Shack takes the family back to basics – there is no television set, only board games, so they lead a simpler life than in London. They love the way the house offers a contrast between their urban existence and life by the water, and readily admit they have the best of both worlds.

BIJOU BATHROOM.
The bathroom is small and functional, with walls covered in white tiles in a variety of different shapes and sizes to keep the small room as light and bright as possible. Above the basin, the taps/faucets are mounted on a worn wooden shelf that resembles a piece of driftwood, adding to the easy-going coastal mood. A delicate black lace curtain hangs at the window to provide privacy (above and left).

BEACHSIDE
hideaway

A pared-down Spanish beach house positioned right at the water's edge.

Nestled in a secluded bay surrounded by rocky cliffs, this typical Spanish fisherman's cabin, built around 60 years ago, sits directly on the beach with a cluster of other whitewashed cottages for company. When Jessica Bataille and Ivan Cristobal bought the property in 2014 to use as their very own private coastal retreat, they knew that they had found a real-life treasure.

The tiny whitewashed house is located in an idyllic spot – looking out at the small island of Portichol, situated just off the south-eastern coast of Spain. Jessica, an interior designer and the owner of Jessica Bataille Lifestyle Company in nearby Javea, knew exactly what she wanted to do with the house and they got to work immediately. A radical renovation was not possible, due to the strict planning laws that apply to coastal properties in Spain, so Jessica and Ivan kept their changes simple, functional and sympathetic to the building's original purpose and surroundings.

A VIEW FROM THE SHORE.
Jessica and Ivan's coastal retreat sits right on the beach and looks out to the nearby island of Portichol (this page). The dining table is positioned to make the most of the view (opposite).

'It's not possible to build houses like this any more, so it's a real gift to own it,' says Jessica.

Jessica created a kitchen area close to the front door with simple whitewashed cabinets and walls enlivened with a splash of turquoise provided by the small window above the sink. The robust terracotta floor tiles are practical, as they can quickly be swept clean of sand and stones and mopped down. However, Jessica says that she would ideally like to swap them for a pebble floor, to keep the house in harmony with its surroundings.

The pared-down colour scheme echoes the views outside the cabin, with white walls and woodwork painted in a vivid turquoise hue. Jessica opted for simple, functional furniture – distressed and worn wooden pieces plus woven natural fibre rugs, lampshades and baskets. The house is not connected to the electricity network, so the family are reliant on solar panels for power. The rattan lampshades are reminiscent of traditional woven lobster pots and bring warmth and texture to the clean white scheme.

When it came to choosing fabrics, Jessica picked washed linen and striped cotton, with the odd pop of brighter colour and pattern in the form of cushions from her store. Accessories and furniture were mostly sourced from local flea markets and Jessica explains that she didn't want to have anything valuable here

MADE BY HAND.
The kitchen is small but perfectly formed. The white-painted cabinets were constructed from bricks and wooden doors, while terracotta floor tiles add warmth to the scheme (opposite). A handmade shelving unit in the dining space houses tableware (right). The woodwork throughout is painted a vibrant tropical turquoise (above right).

– everything was chosen to survive beach living. She's created a relaxed, rustic vibe, mixing and matching wooden chairs and rattan stools with natural fibre rugs. At the kitchen window, a sisal mat doubles as a blind/shade to block sunlight and provide privacy. Simple decorative accents, such as the straw hats on the walls, hint at the coastal location without overplaying it.

Jessica says that her most treasured moments are the early mornings here spent gazing out to sea, which remind her of a Picasso painting of a girl at the water's edge. 'I love to sit at the window and watch the sea,' she explains. 'It's not possible to build houses like this any more, so it's a real gift to own it.'

BAREFOOT LIVING.

Jessica and Ivan's coastal escape is nestled among a cluster of whitewashed fishermen's cabins, all with shutters and woodwork in vibrant shades of blue (above). Rustic wooden stools and a low rattan table outside the front door are the perfect spot from which to watch the world go by.

LINKING ELEMENTS.

A view from the sitting room through to the main bedroom at the back of the cabin (opposite and right). White walls are teamed with terracotta tiles on the floor – a practical choice for a seaside abode. Colour pops of yellow and turquoise recur throughout, and simple patterns add interest to the scheme.

ISLAND *life*

A skilful remodelling using traditional techniques
has resulted in a characterful island home.

ALL SUMMER LONG.
The classic yellow longboard proudly displayed
in the kitchen is testament to Katja's love of
surfing. This open-plan area houses the kitchen
at one end, dining table in the middle and sitting
area at the other (above). Katja and daughter
Florencia spend a great deal of their time
hanging out on the large shady terrace at
the front of the house (opposite).

Katja Wöhr wasn't remotely daunted at the prospect
of renovating a traditional village house in Genova on
the Spanish island of Mallorca. On the contrary, she says
– she feels the house 'was waiting' for her.

In 2014, Katja got her hands on the property and
went straight to work. The house was in a state of total
disrepair with no mains water or electricity and friends
thought she would have to raze it to the ground. Katja
begged to differ, enlisting the help of a specialist
contractor from nearby Formentera to help with the
renovation. The 160-year-old house, typical of the local
architectural style, was originally home to two families,
one living at the end now occupied by Katja's daughter
Florencia, and the other family living in what is now the
main kitchen and living area. The living space was four
small rooms and the kitchen was in the outhouse, which
is now home to the laundry room.

Living off-site but project managing the work, Katja
first hired a crew of Romanian builders. Next came a
team of craftsmen from Formentera to carry out the
more skilled work. The traditional Mallorcan cane ceilings
were made by a craftsman from Campanet. The canes
were sourced from Sóller, in the north of the island,
where they are cut at the time of the full moon in

January when the sap is low, which prevents them from becoming mouldy. To construct the roof, the canes were bound together with jute and covered with paper and a layer of earth before the original pantiles were relaid on top.

The limestone walls were also created by a local craftsperson, Sonja Luna from Barcelona. As the walls have no insulation, the limestone allows them to breathe. Sonja also created the limestone flooring by mixing a Mallorcan cement with various minerals. Using a spatula, the cement was applied to the floor of the dining room and the two bedrooms, a painstaking job that took two people three weeks to finish. The tiles in the kitchen and living areas are the original terracotta flooring.

Katja knew from the start that she wanted a open-plan living space, but says she made a mistake when it came to the bathroom. It was originally going to be situated between her and Florencia's bedrooms, but the builders persuaded her to position it just off the kitchen – a decision that she has come to regret.

The beautiful 1950s French sideboard in the kitchen was spotted in a magazine. As luck would have it, it fitted the space perfectly and Katja snapped it up. It's the most expensive piece in the house, but Katja says it is hugely versatile, holding everything from dried goods to table linen to pots and pans.

Katja has a great eye for detail and is clever when it comes to reclaiming and reusing elements in unexpected ways. The coffee table in the living area was originally a butcher's table

RELAXED RUSTIC.
The muted neutrals of terracotta tiles, rustic linen, rush pouffes, an old wooden table, painted wooden furniture and delicate lace curtains combine to create the most inviting space (opposite and above). The beamed ceiling and chandelier add a note of grandeur, while a dash of aqua is a nod to the house's coastal location.

COLOUR POPS.
The kitchen is peppered with touches of green and limestone walls add subtle texture. The large antique unit that stands along one wall houses everything Katja needs and creates an individual look, making the room more informal and less 'kitchen-like'. Katja painted the shelf unit herself and sourced the beautiful stone sink locally.

but she cut down the legs to make it lower. The kitchen bar came from Katja's store in nearby Santanyí and dates back to the days of her salt farming business, Flor Dé Sal, which she sold to finance the purchase and renovation of the house. The pendant light above the bar is a vintage wine funnel repurposed as a lamp shade and the pretty shelf above the kitchen worksurface was repainted in her favourite colour. Katja worked with a Moroccan carpenter to design and build the kitchen, which is complete with an old stone Mallorcan sink and an island made from wooden pallets. One of her Romanian builders gave her the old bathtub that occupies the end of the bathroom and she found two oak blocks to balance it on. The basin unit was once an old fridge/icebox and the thick linen

curtains that hang in the bedroom were made from the fabric covers of Franciscan monks' beds (similar to old-fashioned camp beds) found in a local antiques shop.

The terrace is home to a medley of mismatched wooden distressed chairs and tables. Katja sourced most of the furniture from local flea markets and the camouflage netting that provides shade from the midday sun is supplied by a German friend and taken down in winter. The fabrics and cushions are a mix of embroidered and striped fabrics produced on the island. 'The fabric never deteriorates, it's such good quality,' Katja explains.

Katja likes to describe her house as a humble abode, but in truth it's a coastal home full of soul, crafted with genuine love, care and attention.

SOAK AND SLEEP.
The bathroom is in the centre of the house (this page). Everything here was tailor-made rather than being 'off the shelf'. The bathtub was a hand-me-down, the basin table was originally a fridge/icebox and even the wonky shower curtain pole makes a charming feature. Plain and patterned tiles add interest.

INTRIGUING TEXTURE.
The heavy-duty loose-weave linen curtains that hang at the French doors are another of Katja's clever ideas. Originally part of a camp bed, you can still see the old buttonholes down the edges that held the fabric to the bed frames.

LOW-LEVEL LIVING.
A shady seating area made from weathered rustic beams and roll-up rattan blinds/shades has been created at the front of the house (opposite). Low-level chairs painted soft blue are piled with linen cushions sourced locally that are perfect for outdoor use.

ALFRESCO STYLE.
The exterior of the house has been whitewashed, while the windows are cleverly framed with a soft grey hue to turn them into a feature (this page). More low-level furniture is piled high with cotton-covered cushions and soft throws to create a laid-back lounging area; it's Mau-Mau the cat's favourite place to hang out.

MALLORCAN
family retreat

Surfers Gerry and Gesine have created an idyllic coastal retreat to call home.

Gesine and Gerry Haag spent many years chasing waves around the world, so the typical Mallorcan house where they have settled (for now) is, of course, inspired by their travels and their mutual love of the ocean. The Haags' home was built in the 1970s of local sandstone and is huddled into a hillside in the small village of Genova. The area boasts narrow, winding roads and traditional architecture, and enjoys panoramic views over the ocean yet is close to Mallorca's elegant, cosmopolitan capital Palma.

SHADY DAYS.
The covered outdoor seating area by the pool features roughly plastered walls and built-in seating piled high with cushions in faded aqua shades.

MALLORCAN STYLE.
In the kitchen, wooden cabinets were painted a rich sea green, then rubbed back to create a distressed effect (below). The colour is echoed in the locally made tiles fitted above the cooker. The whole interior is painted a soft off-white with accents of turquoise, aqua and blue recurring throughout. Elsewhere in the kitchen, the couple chose to retain the original wooden shutters and wall tiles, which add depth and rich tones to the room (left).

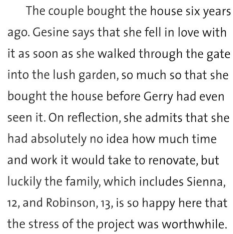

The couple bought the house six years ago. Gesine says that she fell in love with it as soon as she walked through the gate into the lush garden, so much so that she bought the house before Gerry had even seen it. On reflection, she admits that she had absolutely no idea how much time and work it would take to renovate, but luckily the family, which includes Sienna, 12, and Robinson, 13, is so happy here that the stress of the project was worthwhile.

The couple were intent on retaining the original spirit of the house, but wanted to adapt it to fit their lifestyle and make it suitable for year-round use. The interior consisted of a warren of small rooms and tiny windows, so they decided to open it up to connect inside with out and create a large living area in which to cook, eat and relax.

The interior was planned by interior designer Carde Reimerdes of Mallorca-based Seawashed, who also managed the massive rebuild project. Work started on the upper floor first and Gerry and Gesine say that the day the internal walls came down was when they first had an inkling of how the house was going to feel. Steel beams were installed to support the new open-plan structure, the roof was replaced, heating was installed and the house was rewired and connected to the water main.

The couple wanted to create a sociable place where family and friends could come together and sourced two long wooden tables from Seawashed, one for

WATERY HUES.
The open-plan dining area is home to a few carefully chosen coastal-inspired pieces plus natural textures such as bamboo and weathered wood. Pops of vibrant blue and green add colour, while an old longboard pays homage to Gerry and Gesine's love of the ocean.

The guest bedroom is on the ground floor and overlooks the pool. A tranquil space, it's furnished with neutral cottons and linens for a relaxed vibe. Simple roll-up blinds/shades and a mosquito net above the bed add texture and interest (below). The oversized seagrass lampshades in the master bathroom make a dramatic focal point (opposite). A towel rail crafted from driftwood is in keeping with the coastal location (left).

inside and one for the terrace. The dining table is the focal point in the living area. Two beautiful bell-shaped glass lamps in a milky aqua hue hang above it – they remind the couple of the ocean and a visit to Pablo Neruda's house in Chile. 'I love them, as they were handmade in a traditional glass-blowing workshop on the island,' Gesine explains.

The kitchen is at the other end of the living space. It's kitted out with locally made tiles and the cabinets are sea green. The walls are painted a subtle, bleached white and the interior is enlivened with accents of turquoise, green and blue – colours that reflect the couple's passion for the ocean.

The design influences in the house can be traced back to Gesine and Gerry's love of surfing and their travels in Hawaii and Australia, and the living area is home to striking underwater photographs sourced from Bondi Beach in Australia. Gesine points out a very special piece of art by the Maui-based legendary big-wave surfer Pete

Cabrinha that the couple bought on one of their trips. They even factored a 'board room' into the rebuild to store their surfboards and kite-surfing equipment.

One of the couple's favourite rooms is their bedroom. The huge bed was designed by Seawashed and built by a local Moroccan craftsman. Gesine and Gerry can watch the sunrise from bed, and the rest of the family can squeeze in too. The bathroom is a rustic haven, combining a seagrass roof with a pebble floor in the shower area. The rattan pendant lamps were originally fish traps and were transformed by Seawashed for a stylish coastal touch. Plaster walls keep the room bright.

This casual, carefree home is a testament to the Haags' laid-back lifestyle and love of the sea, with areas to kick back, relax and enjoy the views in all directions.

HANGING OUT.
The seating area at one end of the swimming pool is an ideal place to relax with friends and family. Gesine's favourite spot is the swinging double day bed, which was constructed from old wooden pallets and attached to the roof beams with sturdy ropes (above).

UP ON THE ROOF.
Gently distressed paintwork, bleached woods and subtle aqua hues are key to the laid-back style of the Haags' home (right and opposite). On the upstairs terrace is an old metal ladder leading up to the roof. Daughter Sienna painted it different shades of blue and calls it 'the Olympic rings'.

ADDRESS BOOK

WALLPAPERS, FABRICS AND PAINTS

Abigail Edwards Wallpaper
abigailedwards.com
Delicate seascape wallpapers in a variety of soft tones.

Annie Sloan Paints
anniesloan.com
Annie produces chalk paints ideal for painting furniture and upcycling tired pieces of furniture. Visit her website for more details and inspiration on how to use her ingenious paint.

Benjamin Moore Paints
benjaminmoore.com
American company supplying high-quality paint for the home.

Beyond France
beyondfrance.co.uk
Authentic vintage linens, grain sacks and indigo fabrics sourced from all over Europe.

Dash and Albert
dashandalberteurope.com
A huge selection of rugs, accessories, cushions, pouffes and tote bags that can be used both indoor and outdoor and come in a wide variety of colours and designs, including stripes, patterns, and plains.

Earthborn Paints
earthbornpaints.co.uk
Breathable clay paints that are environmentally friendly.

Ian Mankin
ianmankin.co.uk
A huge selection of traditional weaves, stripes, linens, cottons, tickings, ginghams and plain fabrics, all made in the UK.

Jane Churchill Fabrics and Wallpapers
janechurchill.com
A vast array of striped fabrics and wallpapers in a kaleidoscope of shades and designs.

Little Greene
littlegreene.com
Environmentally friendly paints for both interiors and exteriors and available in a vast array of colours.

Parna Ltd
parna.co.uk
Online stockist of vintage linens, cushion covers, striped and hand-embroidered fabrics.

ACCESSORIES

Atlantic Blankets
atlanticblankets.com
Inspired by their surroundings and the British coastline, this family-run business based in Cornwall works with the best mills to make a wonderful selection of throws and blankets.

The Beach Hut
thebeachhut.co.uk
A curated collection of inspiring coastal finds to add to your home, ranging from driftwood accessories to practical bedding and blankets to lighting.

Chart Sales
chartsales.co.uk
Nautical chart suppliers stocking thousands of genuine navigation charts and publications worldwide.

Falcon Enamel
falconenamelware.com
Classic enamel kitchenware that is beautiful and functional and durable with a timeless elegance and in classic colours.

Igigi General Store
igigigeneralstore.com
Brighton-based purveyors of relaxed style, including rustic homewares, baskets, wooden spoons, vintage fabrics, linens, handcrafted items and soaps.

John Lewis
johnlewis.com
Stocks everything from coastal wallpapers and furniture and rattan baskets to lighting, both online and in store.

Kirsty Elson
kirstyelson.co.uk
Delightful driftwood artist based in Cornwall. Her delicate sculptures are unique and charming.

The Lexington Company
lexingtoncompany.com
Everything for the home with an American coastal vibe, ranging from bed linen to dinnerware.

The Linen Works
thelinenworks.co.uk
Luxurious linen bedding, tablecloths and cushion covers in a selection of muted colours.

Maud and Mabel
maudandmabel.com
A tranquil shopping sanctuary dedicated to a diverse selection of textural and handcrafted ceramics, cloth and wooden items made by over forty pioneering artists and makers from the UK, Italy, Scandinavia and Japan.

Merchants of the Sea
merchantsofthesea.com.au
Australian store featuring a wonderful selection of vintage nautical items that speak of a bygone coastal lifestyle. Will ship worldwide.

Molesworth and Bird
molesworthandbird.com
Online coastal shop that describes itself as 'inspired by foraged jewels and treasures from the sea'.

Pedlars Vintage
pedlars.co.uk
Handpicked vintage dealers showcasing a huge variety of homewares, ranging from nautical posters to wooden furniture and storage to traditional kitchenalia.

Ryder and Hope
ryderandhope.com
Sources beautiful homewares and products chosen because of their design, heritage and usefulness. Iconic pieces sit alongside traditional and hand-crafted items.

Sue Pryke
suepryke.com
Beautiful contemporary handmade tableware and ceramics in delicate coastal shades.

Will and Yates
willandyates.com
A coastal gallery and homestore that brings together art and interior styling, original paintings, prints, ceramics, vintage and new decorative pieces.

FURNITURE AND FLOORING

California Shutters
californiashutters.co.uk
Wooden window shutters in all styles and colours to add a dash of coastal style to your windows.

Homebarn
homebarnshop.co.uk
Described as 'The New Curiosity Shop', this vast wooden barn is jam-packed with worn, weathered and rustic style furniture and vintage salvaged pieces along with interesting accessories and lighting.

Kersaint Cobb
kersaintcobb.co.uk
Natural flooring made from seagrass, jute, coir and sisal, bringing the beauty of nature indoors.

Oka
oka.com
A one-stop-shop for faux shells and coral, basketware storage, cotton tablelinen and functional furniture in classic designs including weathered woods and rattan for inside and out.

Pottery Barn
potterybarn.com
US lifestyle store stocking everything from furniture to towels in affordable classic and contemporary designs.

Restoration Hardware
restorationhardware.com
A collection of timeless, updated classics and authentic reproductions including furniture, lighting, textiles, rugs, bathware and accessories.

Roger Oates
rogeroates.com
Authentic flatweave runners and rugs in a large selection of stripes and colour blocks and a selection of colours.

LIGHTING

Davey Lighting
originalbtc.com
Classic lighting company with roots dating back to the 19th century and combining industrial design, craftsmanship and the finest materials. Classic nautical interior and exterior lighting in a variety of finishes.

Garden Trading
gardentrading.co.uk
Contemporary indoor and outdoor lighting along with stylish kitchen accessories, practical homeware, rustic furniture and enamelware.

Louise Tucker Lighting
louisetucker.net
Intricate and beautiful handmade lighting made using a pioneering blend of traditional weaving techniques and contemporary product design.

Urban Archaeology
urbanarchaelogy.com
With a background in architectural salvage, this US company is now also a leading resource for new lighting, bath and kitchen furnishings and even tiles.

Urban Cottage Industries
urbancottageindustries.com
Pioneers of the industrial lighting aesthetic, Urban Cottage stock everything from industrial style outdoor lights to fabric-covered flex/cord to Bakelite accessories and factory-style enamel pendants.

   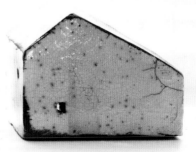

PICTURE CREDITS

1 The home of Lori Guyer, owner of White Flower Farmhouse, in Greenport, New York; 4 Home of Justine Hand, contributing editor at Remodelista, on Cape Cod; 5 left The Ferryman's and The Saltbox are situated on the Elmley Nature Reserve and available to rent www.elmleynaturereserve.co.uk/stay; 5 centre Hannah Childs Interior Design, Old Lyme, CT; 8–9 A house on Long Island designed by Marissa Savarese; 10 above right Elena Colombo; 10 below left 'Albany' in Port Isaac, designed by Nicola O'Mara and available to rent through www.boutique-retreats.co.uk; 10 below right Katja Wöhr; 12 Hannah Childs Interior Design, Old Lyme, CT; 13 left The Shack is available as a shoot location www.lordshippark. com; 13 centre The home of Lori Guyer, owner of White Flower Farmhouse, in Greenport, New York; 13 right The beach hideaway in Javea designed by Jessica Bataille www.jessicabataille.com; 14 left The beach hideaway in Javea designed by Jessica Bataille www.jessicabataille.com; 14 right Elena Colombo; 15 left The beach hideaway in Javea designed by Jessica Bataille www.jessicabataille. com; 16 and 17 below left The Old Coastguard House – home of Martin and Jane Will; 17 above left The Ferryman's and The Saltbox are situated on the Elmley Nature Reserve and available to rent www.elmleynaturereserve.co.uk/stay; 17 below right Katja Wöhr; 20 below right 'Nautilis' is the home in Cornwall of James and Lisa Bligh www.uniquehomestays.com; 22 above left and below A house on Long Island designed by Marissa Savarese; 22 above right The Shack is available as a shoot location www.lordshippark. com; 23 The Old Coastguard House – home of Martin and Jane Will; 25 centre 'Albany' in Port Isaac, designed by Nicola O'Mara and available to rent through www.boutique-retreats.co.uk; 25 right The Old Coastguard House – home of Martin and Jane Will; 26 left The Shack is available as a shoot location www.lordshippark. com; 26 right 'Albany' in Port Isaac, designed by Nicola O'Mara and is available to rent through www.boutique-retreats.co.uk; 27 left The home of conscious entrepreneurs Gesine and Gerry Haag and their kids Sienna and Robinson in Mallorca; 27 right 'Nautilis' is the home in Cornwall of James and Lisa Bligh www.uniquehomestays. com; 28 left and centre The home of conscious entrepreneurs Gesine and Gerry Haag and their kids Sienna and Robinson in Mallorca; 28 right Elena Colombo; 29 The beach hideaway in Javea designed by Jessica Bataille www.jessicabataille.com; 30 above left and below left 'Nautilis' is the home in Cornwall of James and Lisa Bligh www.uniquehomestays.com; 30 above right Elena Colombo; 30 below right The home of Lori Guyer, owner of White Flower Farmhouse, in Greenport, New York; 31 Elena Colombo; 32 above left Katja Wöhr; 32 above right 'Nautilis' is the home in Cornwall of James and Lisa Bligh www.uniquehomestays.com; 32 below left Home of Justine Hand, contributing editor at Remodelista, on Cape Cod; 32 below right The Ferryman's and The Saltbox are situated on the Elmley Nature Reserve and available to rent www. elmleynaturereserve.co.uk/stay; 33 The home of Lori Guyer, owner of White Flower Farmhouse, in Greenport, New York; 34 The home of conscious entrepreneurs Gesine and Gerry Haag and their kids Sienna and Robinson in Mallorca; 35 left The Ferryman's and The Saltbox are situated on the Elmley Nature Reserve and available

to rent www.elmleynaturereserve.co.uk/stay; 35 right Home of Justine Hand, contributing editor at Remodelista, on Cape Cod; 36 left and right The home of conscious entrepreneurs Gesine and Gerry Haag and their kids Sienna and Robinson in Mallorca; 36 centre The Shack is available as a shoot location www.lordshippark. com; 37 'Nautilis' is the home in Cornwall of James and Lisa Bligh www.uniquehomestays.com; 38 above left 'Nautilis' is the home in Cornwall of James and Lisa Bligh www.uniquehomestays.com; 38 above right Elena Colombo; 38 below left The Old Coastguard House – home of Martin and Jane Will; 38 below right The Ferryman's and The Saltbox are situated on the Elmley Nature Reserve and available to rent www.elmleynaturereserve.co.uk/stay; 39 and 40 left 'Albany' in Port Isaac, designed by Nicola O'Mara and available to rent through www.boutique-retreats.co.uk; 40 right The Ferryman's and The Saltbox are situated on the Elmley Nature Reserve and available to rent www.elmleynaturereserve.co.uk/stay; 41 left The beach hideaway in Javea designed by Jessica Bataille www. jessicabataille.com; 41 right The Old Coastguard House – home of Martin and Jane Will; 42 The beach hideaway in Javea designed by Jessica Bataille www.jessicabataille.com; 43 The home of Lori Guyer, owner of White Flower Farmhouse, in Greenport, New York; 44 The Old Coastguard House – home of Martin and Jane Will; 45 above left The home of Lori Guyer, owner of White Flower Farmhouse, in Greenport, New York; 45 below centre 'Albany' in Port Isaac, designed by Nicola O'Mara and available to rent through www. boutique-retreats.co.uk; 45 below right The Old Coastguard House – home of Martin and Jane Will; 46–47 left The home of Lori Guyer, owner of White Flower Farmhouse, in Greenport, New York; 48 The home of conscious entrepreneurs Gesine and Gerry Haag and their kids Sienna and Robinson in Mallorca; 48 right 'Nautilis' is the home in Cornwall of James and Lisa Bligh www.uniquehomestays.com; 49 Hannah Childs Interior Design, Old Lyme, CT; 50 'Nautilis' is the home in Cornwall of James and Lisa Bligh www.uniquehomestays. com; 51 above left The Ferryman's and The Saltbox are situated on the Elmley Nature Reserve and available to rent www. elmleynaturereserve.co.uk/stay; 51 below left and right 'Albany' in Port Isaac, designed by Nicola O'Mara and available to rent through www.boutique-retreats.co.uk; 54–63 'Albany' in Port Isaac, designed by Nicola O'Mara and available to rent through www. boutique-retreats.co.uk; 64–71 The Ferryman's and The Saltbox are situated on the Elmley Nature Reserve and available to rent www.elmleynaturereserve.co.uk/stay; 72–81 'Nautilis' is the home in Cornwall of James and Lisa Bligh www.uniquehomestays.com; 82–91 Home of Justine Hand, contributing editor at Remodelista, on Cape Cod; 92–99 Elena Colombo; 100–109 Hannah Childs Interior Design, Old Lyme, CT; 110–119 A house on Long Island designed by Marissa Savarese; 120–127 The home of Lori Guyer, owner of White Flower Farmhouse, in Greenport, New York; 128–133 The Old Coastguard House – home of Martin and Jane Will; 136–143 The Shack is available as a shoot location www.lordshippark.com; 146–151 The beach hideaway in Javea designed by Jessica Bataille www.jessicabataille.com; 152–161 Katja Wöhr; 162–169 The home of conscious entrepreneurs Gesine and Gerry Haag and their kids Sienna and Robinson in Mallorca; 170–171 The Old Coastguard House – home of Martin and Jane Will; 176 The Ferryman's and The Saltbox are situated on the Elmley Nature Reserve and available to rent www.elmleynaturereserve.co.uk/stay.

BUSINESS CREDITS

Carde Reimerdes Seawashed
Design/Furniture/Art
Calle Pinaret nº05
07184 Calviá
Mallorca
T: +34 659 70 24 23
E: contactme@seawashed.eu
seawashed.eu
Pages 27 left, 28 left, 28 centre, 34, 36 left, 36 right, 48, 162–169.

The Ferryman's and The Saltbox
T: +44 (0)7930 847520
E: stay@elmleynature reserve.co.uk
elmleynaturereserve.co.uk/stay
and
Huts made by
Plankbridge
Master Hut Makers
www.plankbridge.com
and
Blankets and throws from
Romney Marsh Wools
romneymarshwools.co.uk
and
Soft furnishings by
Fable & Base
fableandbase.co.uk

Pages 5 left, 17 above left, 32 below right, 35 left, 38 below right, 40 right, 51 above left, 64–71, 176.

Fire Features
Colombo Construction Corp
342 Park Avenue
Brooklyn
New York, NY 11205
T: +1 718 399 2233
E: info@firefeatures.com
firefeatures.com
Pages 10 above right, 14 right, 28 right, 30 above right, 31, 38 above right, 92–99.

Hannah Childs Interior Design
Old Lyme, CT 06371
T: +1 860 405 4394
E: info@hannahchilds interiordesign.com
hannahchildsinterior design.com
and
Allee Architecture + Design
5916 North Elm Avenue
Millerton, NY 12546
T: +1 860 435 0640
E: info@alleedesign.com
alleedesign.com
Pages 5 centre, 12, 49, 100–109.

Katja Wöhr
Pages 10 below right, 17 below right, 32 above left, 152–161.

Marissa Savarese Design
New York and Zurich
E: marissa.savarese@gmail.com
and

Mark Schwartz & Associates
28495 Main Road
Cutchogue, NY 11935
T: +1 631 734 4185
E: info@mksarchitect.com
mksarchitect.com
and
Thomas Sanders
T.S. Custom Carpentry Inc.
26481 Main Road
Cutchogue, NY 11935
T: +1 631 956 2396
Pages 8–9, 22 above left, 22 below, 110–119.

Nicola O'Mara Interior Design
Swallows Park
St Minver
Wadebridge
Cornwall PL27 6PQ
T: +44 (0)1208 863 716
E: mail@nicolaomara.com
nicolaomara.com
Pages 10 below left, 25 centre, 26 right, 39, 40 left, 45 below centre, 51 below left, 54–63.

Studio Jessica Bataille
Calle Bruselas 8
03730 Javea
Alicante, Spain
jessicabataille.com
Pages 13 right, 14 left, 15 left, 29, 41 left, 42, 146–151.

The Shack
lordshippark.com
Pages 13 left, 22 above right, 26 left, 36 centre, 136–143.

Unique Home Stays
T: +44 (0)1637 881183
uniquehomestays.com
Unique Home Stays
Interior designer Jess Clark
Pages 20 below right, 27 right, 30 above left, 30 below left, 32 above right, 37, 38 above left, 48 right, 50, 72–81.

White Flower Farmhouse
53995 Main Road
Southold, NY 11971
E: whiteflowershop@aol.com
Instagram: whiteflowerfarmhouse
Pages 1, 13 centre, 30 below right, 33, 43, 45 above left, 46, 47 left, 120–127.

Will and Yates Gallery + Homestore
Paintings, furniture and vintage homewares
95 Beach Street
Deal
Kent CT14 6JE
T: +44 (0)1304 374700
willandyates.com
Pages 16, 17 below left, 23, 25 right, 38 below left, 41 right, 44, 45 below right, 128–133, 170–171.

INDEX

Page numbers in italic refer to the illustrations

ACKNOWLEDGMENTS

Firstly, a very big thank you to Ryland Peters & Small, who commissioned me to style and write this book. Thank you everyone for believing in me, especially Jess, and a special thank you also to Megan, who worked through every single layout with me to make the book look its best.

Secondly, a huge thank you to Benjamin Edwards: a top-notch photographer who not only takes beautiful photos but also shares my love of a decent cup of tea. Thank you!

We did a lot of travelling to photograph this book and it was an honour and a privilege to work in some truly beautiful places. Special thanks go to Katja, Carde and Gesine – so welcoming and special. It was a joy to meet you all and hopefully we'll meet again. Thanks also to Lori, with her warm, welcoming heart, who took time out to show us her home, introduced us to New York pizza pie and showed us hidden gems in her local area. Also Justine, Elena, Jessica, Hannah and Sian and Stuart, who let us into their stunning homes and spent precious time with us, and to all the other wonderful owners for sharing their inspiring coastal interiors.

I'd also like to take this opportunity to thank my followers on Instagram, who indirectly helped this book come to life, and anyone who has supported my work as a stylist over the last twenty years – it means the world to me.

Last but certainly not least, I would like to thank my gorgeous family. My husband plays the role of both mum and dad when I'm working and does the best job in the world. You are my rock and my love. Thanks to my boys, who I love more than life itself, and who keep me laughing on a daily basis. And to my Mum, whose unconditional love and support has kept me going through thick and thin. Lastly, I would like to dedicate this book to my lovely late Dad, himself a Master Mariner, who instilled in me a love of being in and by the sea.